Alexander Dru was born in England in 1904 and attended the Downside School and Cambridge University. His previous works include *Péguy* and noted translations of Kierkegaard's *Journals* and the *Letters* of Jacob Burckhardt. He is also a contributor to *Downside Review*.

THE CONTRIBUTION OF
GERMAN CATHOLICISM

IS VOLUME

101

OF THE

Twentieth Century Encyclopedia of Catholicism

UNDER SECTION

IX

THE CHURCH AND THE MODERN WORLD

IT IS ALSO THE

109TH

VOLUME IN ORDER OF PUBLICATION

Edited by *HENRI DANIEL-ROPS* *of the Académie Française*

THE CONTRIBUTION OF
GERMAN CATHOLICISM

By ALEXANDER DRU

HAWTHORN BOOKS · PUBLISHERS · *New York*

First Edition, October, 1963

NIHIL OBSTAT

Joannes M. T. Barton, S.T.D., L.S.S.

Censor Deputatus

IMPRIMATUR

Georgius L. Craven

Episcopus Sebastopolis, Vic. Cap.

Westmonasterii, die XXIX JULLI MCMLXIII

H-9546

CONTENTS

EDITOR'S NOTE

The Contribution of German Catholicism fulfills a dual role in the series. On the one hand, it reviews the main events in the Church's development in Germany from 1800 to 1918, emphasizing the cultural and intellectual spheres rather than political events. On the other hand, by comparing and contrasting the Catholic situation in Germany with that in France, it casts a new and challenging light on the Church's mission in the modern world.

As a result of the French Revolution, the traditional union between Church and State was shattered. But, as the author points out, the leaders of the Church in post-Revolutionary France, decided to return to the old position of dependence on the State, thus engaging French Catholicism in a long, sterile struggle with the State and the nation. German Catholic thinkers of the romantic movement, however, rejected this form of "political" Catholicism and sought to develop a "religious" Catholicism based on the realities of their time. The influence of these thinkers was later obscured, but it was revived after World War I and it continues to provide a deeply spiritual tradition both for German Catholics and the Church in the West.

The Contribution of German Catholicism takes up, from a different angle and with new insights, problems and situations discussed in the following volumes in the series: Volume 79, *The Church in the Eighteenth Century;* Volume 88, *The Catholic Spirit;* Volume 89, *Church and State;* Volume 102, *The Church's Mission in the World;* and Volume 119, *Modern Christian Literature.*

INTRODUCTION

The history of the Church since the French Revolution is
commonly projected on a two-dimensional plane which allows
of a detailed and accurate map whose co-ordinates are Church
and State, religion and politics, Rome and Paris. Anything
which falls outside those terms of reference is either omitted,
or treated as subsidiary in the sense of having no decisive
influence on the principle theme. The French Revolution is
then regarded as primarily political and appears as gravely
compromising or threatening the "normal" relations of Church
and State. From 1800 to 1914 the policy of the authorities
of Catholicism was in fact framed in these terms, and it can
therefore be said that history was to some extent made and
written in the same key. The outstanding figure on this
two-dimensional map is the Abbé de Lamennais, whether as
a reactionary (1817–28) or as a liberal (1828–34). In this
framework the "religious question" means the politico-
religious question and any other view is exceptional, almost
eccentric.[1] That is why the Kulturkampf is the only episode in
the history of the Church of Germany which receives attention: because it fits into the *fable convenue*. This conventional
side-glance at the German scene is not only defective through
being incomplete, it not only distorts the history of the Church
in Germany, but prevents a distinct view of the history of the

[1] Henri Bremond, reviewing P. de la Gorce's *Histoire religieuse de
la Révolution Française*, comments on the title: *"Religious History"*,
that is to say, contrary to inveterate custom, the history of the religious life, the history of grace in souls, and not external, political,
superficial history .. " (*Annale de Phil. Chrétienne*, vol. xv, p. 81,
1912).

Church as a whole. In order to embrace the German scene the framework itself needs to be expanded, and this makes it possible to see the period as a whole.

For the Revolution, as it occurred in Germany, was primarily cultural and social, not political. The political Revolution was contained by Metternich; the monarchies and particularist States survived until 1918. The fundamental changes occurred in the cultural sphere. The Revolution certainly destroyed the pre-revolutionary structure of the Church as effectively in Germany as in France, but the political life of the country was not interrupted, the nation was not divided against itself, and the revolution which the Church had to face was cultural, affecting the spheres of thought, manners and morals, of philosophy and history, science and art. In order to embrace the German scene in the history of the Church as a whole it is therefore necessary to include the third dimension in history, to add the sphere of culture to those of religion and politics, so that the "religious question" is seen as a whole, in the round and not only from the political angle. Once this wider aperture is used, the inadequacy of the conventional picture becomes obvious. For the Revolution in France was not essentially different from the Revolution in Germany, though events may make it seem so.

The unity of the period is unmistakable: where the Church is concerned, the Revolution marked *the end of Christendom*; it was the moment in a long process when the Church was faced with an unprecedented situation. Until 1789, the Church had been a power on a par with the State, both of which were englobed in a cultural whole, Christendom. This situation—the *ancien régime*—had been profoundly modified at the Reformation; but while the cultural unity of the past was split, the relations between Church and State were largely unaffected. The Renaissance State-Churches, Catholic and Protestant, perpetuated externally, though under different forms, the relationship which had existed in Christendom. The

Erastian Churches modified the previous conception but did not alter it essentially: and they were in effect a pragmatic answer to a *de facto* situation. But in the post-revolutionary era the State underwent a further transformation—influenced once again by culture—and the formula adopted at the end of the Wars of Religion (1648), *cujus regio, ejus religio*, though still politically advantageous, ceased to be practicable for cultural reasons. The "liberal", post-revolutionary State became "indifferent" to the religion of its "subjects" who had become "the people".

The cultural effect of the Revolution was not at first admitted either by the Church or by the States, all of which desired, as far as possible, to restore the *ancien régime* and to use the forces of religion to contain the Revolution. The authorities of Catholicism, failing to understand the significance of the cultural revolution, hoped to profit from an alliance with the restored monarchies in order to make good the losses incurred at the Revolution. "Indifference" was condemned, and the new situation created by the Revolution, or at least disclosed by it, was rejected in theory and in practice. This point of view became the basis of Church policy until 1914. But after 1848 the difficulties of reconciling policy and situation steadily increased, and some form of compromise became necessary. This was achieved when the full restatement of the Church's policy, the *Syllabus of Errors*, was published in 1864. Recourse was had to a distinction; the *thesis* governing Church policy was fully maintained, and this amounted in fact to adhering to the view that "Christendom" was the only admissible situation for the Church. But since it did not exist everywhere, certain concessions and accommodations could be allowed on the basis of the *hypothesis*: that Christendom did not exist. The opportunism of this escape clause did much to envenom the relations between the Church and the States which were by then, with rare exceptions, "indifferent", and it created an "image" of the Church which divorced it from the people and prevented any links with the culture of the period.

The conflict between the Church and "the Revolution" which followed, and is known as the Kulturkampf in Germany, was not, however, a natural or inevitable development beyond the Rhine. The situation of the Church of Germany had been unique from the first—as unlike that of the Latin countries as that of the Church in America. Since the Council of Trent it had lived in a different world, belonging to the diaspora, at once intimately linked by its institutions to the Empire, yet without conforming, except superficially, to the model of an Erastian Church. This confused situation allowed of a degree of independence, and because its relations with the State were in practice indeterminate, the Church in Germany was able to re-establish its relations with the culture of the times. Once freed by the secularization of the ecclesiastical lands from its anachronistic institutions, the German Church did not react against the political revolution but showed its continued vitality by recognizing the cultural revolution, as the necessary preliminary to fulfilling its mission. Where the Church of France settled into reaction, the Church of Germany experienced a spiritual and intellectual renaissance—a rejuvenation for which there is no place in the conventional historical framework, because it was independent of the relations of Church and State. But the history of the German Church is not merely the history of an outlying province. It throws the problems before the Church as a whole into relief, and its inclusion reveals the pattern which allows the unity of Church history since the Revolution to be seen.

The unity of the history of the Church since the revolution can be thrown into relief by considering the three phases in which the Church faced the situation created by the Revolution.

The first phase opens in France with a double event: the

publication of the Napoleonic concordat and of Chateaubriand's *Le Génie du Christianisme* in 1802, indicating the
alternative policies before the Church: either a return to a
contrived alliance between Church and State, or reliance on
an untried medium, culture, involving recognition of the new
situation. The second solution was successfully pursued in
Germany, but in France it was crippled from birth by
Napoleon's determination to re-establish an Erastian Church
as being the essential buttress of "order". It is at this point
that the German story throws a fresh light on the French
scene—by throwing the importance of the cultural sphere into
relief. For it was Napoleon who deliberately, and effectively, strangled the romantic movement in France at birth.
With Mme de Staël in exile throughout the Emperor's reign,
and with Chateaubriand in opposition and without influence,
the romantic movement, which in Germany provided the
religious revival with wings, was fatally arrested in its development. In consequence, the religious revival was channelled
towards old forms, towards a political conception of religion
falling back into the hands of men belonging to the previous
age and generation, into the hands of Bonald and Maistre,
born in the middle of the eighteenth century, whose classicism
was innate and whose static view of things was already pre-
historic. The quarrel between Pope and Emperor, and the ill-
treatment to which Napoleon subjected Pius VII only fur-
thered this tendency, and with the return of the Bourbons
in 1815 the stage was set for the hundred years war between
Church and State once the "Catholic" monarchy disappeared.
The "religious question" as it developed in France was the
consequence of excluding the genuine religious problems: the
result of attempting to settle the problems in the political
arena, where they no longer belonged. Moreover in that
political setting the whole tradition of the Church (still acting
as a "power") was inevitably reactionary, and this powerful

tendency was legally re-enforced by the concordat linking it to the chariot of the Bourbons.

It was during the Bourbon restoration (1815–30) that the decision was reached and the leadership of the Catholic movement was transferred from the hands of Chateaubriand to the hands of Bonald. Chateaubriand saw very clearly that any attempt to impose religion would be met with contempt and loathing. He believed that liberty of conscience was not only desirable in itself but the only possible policy. The authorities of Catholicism and the reactionaries led by Bonald dreamed of happier times when the law, wealth and influence could be brought to bear, and they did not draw the line at the Revocation of the Edict of Nantes. Chateaubriand, on the contrary, whose conservatism was as pliant, realistic and romantic as Disraeli's, placed his confidence in liberty, and it would be true to say that the failure of the liberal Catholic movement in France could be traced back to Chateaubriand's defeat and to his mistakes. For, as Acton wrote to Lady Blennerhasset (in 1894): "It is he who inaugurated the Catholic liberal movement in France, and a good part of their baggage comes from him, whereas he, it seems to me, drew his doctrine from nowhere if not from his changing career. He precedes Lamennais by three or four years." Chateaubriand's doctrine is implicit in *Le Génie du Christianisme*, though Acton was too blind to the aesthetic doctrine in which it was contained to discover it. But whether the Catholic liberal movement is sought in Chateaubriand or in the works of his friends Joubert or Ballanche, it was in the works of men sympathizing with the aims of the romantic movement and who deplored, like Joubert and Ballanche, the narrow, legalistic conception of religion advocated by Bonald and Maistre which they knew would never commend itself to the generation born and brought up in the post-revolutionary world.

Chateaubriand was the only man of his time in France with the authority to advocate the liberal point of view in romantic terms because he appreciated the nature of the cultural revolution no less than the consequences of the political revolution. But his liberalism made him suspect to the reactionaries, and his conservatism to the doctrinaire liberals. Bonald and Lamennais detested his advocacy of constitutional monarchy on the English pattern, and, pleading that only absolute monarchy was genuinely Catholic, worked to undermine his position. With the assistance of a secret society (*Les Chevaliers de la Foi*) Chateaubriand was kept from power until the summer of 1825 and his triumph as foreign minister was short-lived. Under the leadership of Bonald and Lamennais the Catholic party, which had profited from the favourable opinion in which religion had been welcomed back, rapidly fell into disrepute and the hysterical anticlericalism, which was to play a decisive part in French politics for the rest of the century, sprang fully armed into existence—as it still seems to some, inexplicably.

By 1828 the position had worsened to such a degree that Lamennais was driven to reverse all his former opinions—and subsequently came to appreciate Chateaubriand's wisdom. His real claim to fame rests on the next three or four years, during which he created liberal Catholicism. But Lamennais had only changed sides and fundamentally still adhered to the philosophy of Bonald—which is to say that he took a political and sociological view of religion, and though anxious to raise the intellectual level of the clergy his amateurish philosophy and lack of intellectual discipline totally unfitted him for the task. Liberal Catholicism in France continued to suffer from the defects of its founder, so that it was not until the last quarter of the century that the French Church came alive intellectually.

During the first phase, then, the Catholic revival in France, favoured and supported by the ideas of the romantic movement, seemed for a moment as though it might follow the path taken in Germany. But drawn by the Concordat into close relations with the State under Napoleon, and as the religion of the State falling into the hands of the reactionaries during the Bourbon restoration, Catholicism, except for a minority of liberal-minded Catholics, became involved in a hundred years war with the state and the nation. The only exception was the moment, during the Second Empire, when the Church, for the sake of temporary advantages, ignobly supported Napoleon III. Of this phase Tocqueville wrote to Montalembert: "There is nothing to surprise or pain me in the fact that the journalistic *canaille* (Veuillot, etc.) should have thrown themselves at the feet of the new master; it is a natural evolution. But the black ingratitude towards liberty, so shameful a retraction, such base flattery on the part of the preceptors of morals, the guardians of dignity and of true greatness—that really is too much!"[2]

The second phase opens with the Revolution of 1848 and the *volte-face* by Pius IX. From then on the authorities of Catholicism used every means and seized every opportunity to impose their policy uniformly in France and in Germany. This manoeuvre culminated in the Syllabus of 1864, which represents the high-water mark of authoritarianism and clericalism. It is the period of the *Kulturkampf* and the Catholic ghetto.

The third phase covers the years during which the Church as a whole extricated itself from the impasse into which it had allowed itself to be driven: a prolonged crisis involving the abandonment of the policy inaugurated by the Concordat —and in the wake of which we live. It was signalled at the turn of the century by the condemnation of Americanism (1899): of the attitude and outlook which had come into being in a country where the Church had never had, and never could have, more than administrative relations with the State, and

[2] The letter is quoted by Lecanuet in *Annales de Phil. Chrét.* Oct.-Mars 1910–11, p. 128. It was published in answer to the biography of Dom Guéranger by Dom Delatte.

which appeared as a dangerous example of "a free Church in a free State", of the aims of the liberal Catholics. It was this aspect, and not the supposed "heresy" that raised the storm in a teacup which preluded the crisis.

In retrospect it is possible to see that the third phase was in fact a return to the first, to the moment when the Church would have to choose between the alternative policies, which had now been clarified by experience: between an integral political Catholicism (represented by the *Action Française* movement) and a movement as yet uncertain of its future, but which was neither the old liberalism of Lamennais, Montalembert, Acton and Döllinger, nor the new Modernism of Loisy and Tyrrell, but which was becoming conscious of its tasks in the new situation and in the light of the intuitions of the romantic Catholics. It was the period when Möhler, Newman and Rosmini were discovered.

The unity of the history of the Church since the Revolution is contained by those two moments: between the romantic revival and the Catholic renewal at the beginning of the nineteenth century, and the renaissance of Catholicism and romanticism at the beginning of the twentieth century. In between lies the period of hesitation, tension and conflict before the abandonment of the thesis that Christendom represented the only possible situation for the Church. Until that unity could be seen, until the movement at the beginning of the present century had become articulate, the history of German Catholicism during the romantic period was irrelevant, and remained an isolated and subsidiary episode, a field for specialist or amateur. But once the concordat policy broke down the significance of the earlier period became evident. "The study of the intellectual history of Germany at the beginning of the nineteenth century is more than an academic exercise," Philipp Funk wrote in 1929, "it touches on the living questions of the present." In France Blondel had been conscious of taking up his task where "Chateaubriand's musical prelude" broke off.

It is the aim of this essay to present a brief account of the Church in Germany during these three phases. The inclusion of the cultural sphere is its first condition. The extent and complexity of the material to be embraced will explain the selective method used, and in particular the prominence given to the romantic movement—without which the history of the Church remains unintelligible. Moreover the limits of the present series have obliged me to reduce the politico-ecclesiastical history to a bare minimum in order to make room for the cultural history, particularly in the earlier years of the period and down to 1848 when political Catholicism began to emerge. For the unity of the whole period only appears if the initial efforts and achievements of the romantic Catholics are presented so that they can be seen to have been the result of a clear understanding that the Church–State relationship could no longer provide the setting in which Catholic action could be defined, unless the Church were to abandon its mission and withdraw into a cultural ghetto. The alternative was not liberal or conservative Catholicism, but the rejection or recognition of the situation created by the Revolution. This was finally and officially conceded by the Church as a whole when political Catholicism was condemned under the name of the *Action Française* in 1926, the Lateran Treaty was signed and the Temporal Power abandoned. From then on the thesis that Christendom defined the situation of the Church could be forgotten, and the realities governing the fulfilment of the Church's mission throughout the world could be recognized.

CHAPTER I

THE REICHSKIRCHE AND THE SECULARIZATION

At first sight the Reichskirche, at the end of the eighteenth century, seems to conform to the ecclesiastical fashion of the age and to differ in no essentials from the pattern of the Latin countries. Indeed, to the disapproving eye, it appears more decadent; its anachronisms were more glaring, its wealth greater, its privileges more extensive, its *décor* more sumptuous than elsewhere. It not only owned but ruled, forming an integral part of the empire. Its metropolitans were electors, its suffragans vice-regents, its abbots and abbesses governors, while its sinecures supplied the greater and lesser nobility with incomes, "to each according to his need". But the externals are in some important respects misleading. The Reichskirche was not, and never had been, a State Church in the modern meaning of the term. Its rulers were independent and its traditions were alive.

By the Peace of Westphalia (1648) its possessions had been drastically reduced, by nearly half; and what remained were broken up and scattered, large portions becoming an archipelago of Catholic islands in a Lutheran and Calvinist sea. While the Gallican Church was being centralized under Richelieu and Louis XIV, and isolated as the Huguenots were driven into exile, the Reichskirche underwent the opposite process. It was further decentralized, forced to live in close proximity with other denominations and in cultural surroundings that were sometimes alien to its way of life or beliefs. Catholicism in Germany was exposed to a number of dangers, but these did not include isolation, stagnation or complacency. Neither clergy nor laity could hope to seal themselves off successfully from the trend of the times or become separated from the nation. Something of the complexity of the medieval structure survived in the confusion, something of its freedom in the diversity, and to an extent greater than elsewhere the Church preserved its "ancient lights" in the new enlightenment.

This was facilitated by the independence of its rulers, by the rivalry between electors, bishops and canons, between monastery and university, and the network of precedents, claims and rights which held absolutism in its grasp. The impulse given by the Counter-Reformation lingered on; the Jesuit style took on a new lease of life and was naturalized into the German Baroque. By the middle of the eighteenth century the evidence of a continued vitality everywhere met the eye. The whole appearance of parts of Germany was transformed as the Baroque style spread north from the metropolitan see of Salzburg. Cathedrals, village churches, episcopal residences and shrines, monasteries and convents were built, rebuilt or decorated in a style that dazzled by its movement, invention and splendour and that disconcerts by its fusion of the naïf and the sophisticated that are as inextricably mixed as worldly and spiritual. The Baroque was not of the people or by the people, but it was for the people, and through it "the Church restored by force the bond with the popular imagination, and pomp became the predominating feature of the Baroque".[1] The sumptuous church and the exhibitionist *Kaisersaal* were not then museum pieces, but the scenes of a vigorous life, further expressed and called forth by the music of the Mann-

[1] Burckhardt: *Reflections on History*, p. 130.

heim school, of Haydn and Mozart. Until the end of the century, it is true, Catholics played little or no part in the literary life of the country, and it was said that "poetry was a Protestant dialect". Nevertheless, the late Baroque culture of Catholic Germany was spontaneous and general, a sign, which it is easy to underrate, that tradition was alive.

It is a very partial view of the Church of this period which concentrates upon the anti-curial ecclesiology of Febronius, or the Erastian mania of Joseph II, so that they appear as forms of Gallicanism beyond the Rhine. In the first place the ambitions of the electors of Cologne, Mainz and Trier, and of the metropolitan of Salzburg ran counter to those of the emperor. The more enlightened the prince-bishop, the less he wished for interference, whether from emperor or nuncio. The ecclesiastical ruler was not gravely interested in theology, and his anti-Roman policy was essentially a derivative of the desire to increase his administrative control, often in the interests of a more enlightened absolutism. The organization of religion within the Empire was already atrophied, and the real question was not how it could be buttressed in the interests of prince-bishop or emperor, but whether it could be jettisoned without compromising the religious life of the country. By the time the ecclesiastical electors met at Ems (1786) to concert their anti-Roman policy, the decisions which counted for the future were already out of their hands and were being made in the cultural sphere. Cardinal Pacca's despondency, as he travelled down the Rhine, was by no means unjustified, but his reports were written as from Rome, and he judged the condition of the Church by its prince-bishops, and its prince-bishops in the light of France. Of the living tradition of Catholicism in Germany he was ill-placed to form any idea; nor could it be judged except in the light of the test which it was about to undergo.

The Church in Germany was supremely fortunate in experiencing a bloodless revolution. The Reichskirche was not violently overturned, but legally buried; in part because circumstances favoured a peaceful end, but also because it had not been passionately hated. For in an age when the sale of mercenaries was a recognized method of raising revenue, "life under the crozier was good". Almost before the Revolution touched Germany the secularization of the ecclesiastical lands began. The work begun at Campo Formio (1799) and Lunéville (1801) was completed by the *Reichsdeputationshauptschluss* of Regensburg in 1803; and the pre-revolutionary Church ceased to exist with the Holy Roman Empire of the German Nation, the central pillar of Western Christendom.

The Secularization takes the place of the Revolution and the Napoleonic Concordat, and its consequences were diametrically opposite. There was no tragic breach with the past; there was never any possibility of a "restoration". No one desired to reinstate the prince-bishops. The new situation was legally proclaimed and peacefully accepted, and the life of the Church was not fatally interrupted. On the contrary, the destruction of the entire visible structure, the dispersal of its wealth, the abrogation of its privileges, the suppression of the monasteries and universities, the disorganization of the hierarchy, was a blessing in disguise; temporal loss was balanced by spiritual gain. In France, perhaps, but for the Concordat and the re-establishment of the Church, the position would have deteriorated still further, for the Gallican Church was moribund behind its imposing façade. But in Germany the absence of an established ecclesiastical order— which lasted for twenty years—forced the Church back on its spiritual resources and allowed it time to face the new situation unencumbered by an organization conceived for the *ancien régime*. The suppression of the sixteen Catholic universities may be lamented, yet if anything is certain it is that the achievements of the next century owe a heavy debt to the Catholic faculties of theology in Protestant or mixed universities which replaced them. The Church in Germany did not lose touch with the people or with new ideas. The intellectual stagnation produced by the Napoleonic concordat was avoided, and not being tied to a reactionary régime, the Church could prepare itself to face the social problems of the coming age. The Catholic revival in Germany was not canalized into "the religious question" or circumscribed by politico-ecclesiastical problems; and liberated by the secularization it grew in strength, while at one time there were only five bishops in Germany.

- The secularization carried the process of mixing Catholic and Protestant populations a stage further. After 1803 there were no purely Catholic lands. Bavaria received Ansbach and Bayreuth; the Rhineland, three-quarters Catholic, went to Prussia; Württemberg engulfed half a dozen abbeys and principalities that were Catholic; and Baden became a mixed state. The *cujus regio, ejus religio* of 1648 made way for the *Paritätsstaat* of 1815: the Church and the Churches were legally on the same footing. The concordats subsequently agreed between the states and the papacy (Bavaria 1817, the first, Austria 1855 the last) were legal instruments which determined the status and administrative freedom of the Church—not as in France, the basis of policy.[2]

The past history of the Reichskirche, no less than the Secularization predisposed Catholics to see and to accept the situation created by the Revolution and not to view it solely from the political angle, from which it appeared wholly destructive. In the notebooks of J. M. Sailer, afterwards Bishop of Regensburg, and one of the fathers of the Catholic revival, the Revolutionary changes occurring were clearly seen as involving all three dimensions: Culture, the State and the Church. "The philosophical ferment in Germany; the outbreak of the Revolution in France; and the suppression of the Jesuits"—for Sailer was writing before the Secularization,

[2] Relations between Prussia and the Holy See were regulated by the Bull *De Salute Animarum*, 1821.

and his reference to the Jesuits should be interpreted to mean the disappearance of the old ecclesiastical order. Among the generation coming to maturity at the beginning of the nineteenth century, there were many who saw the changes from all sides, as a revolution in the relations of State, Church and Culture. And until 1848 it was "the philosophical ferment" which chiefly engaged their attention, while the politico-ecclesiastical questions, though they might be of primary importance, were viewed in that new light.

CHAPTER II

THE CULTURAL BACKGROUND

In France the Revolution was primarily political and it divided the nation. In Germany it was first and foremost a cultural metamorphosis, a sort of second Reformation, which unified the nation even before it achieved economic and political unity. The fact that Germany possessed no historical, administrative or geo-political centre, no capital, gave literature and thought at this period a specific rôle; they became the medium of unification. This national movement began as the country recovered from the Thirty Years War, working up to a climax which lasted from about 1770 to 1830, from the Storm and Stress period to the death of Hegel (1831). For sixty years the intellectual life of Germany was at or near boiling point, and the national genius flowered as it had done in France in the seventeenth century—only that it was not classical but romantic. It was a great age in letters, poetry, philosophy, music and *Wissenschaft*; and a period of political nullity. It forms a single, unbroken process of regeneration in which Germany became conscious of itself. Nowhere else in Europe was the transformation as complete and uninterrupted, so global and synthetic. Elsewhere the cultural transformation involved a break or a revolution between the age of Enlightenment and the Romantic period. In Germany it was a continuous evolution; the one merges into the other, and the Enlightenment was deepened until it became the romantic renaissance.

There was only one respect in which the tendency of the past could be said to have been reversed. The Age of Reason threatened to make the split in the European tradition absolute, and to divorce religion and culture. In Germany the threat in its old form was temporarily halted and the romantic movement was intimately associated with the religious revival. "The revolution which has occurred in the minds of thinking men in Germany during the last thirty years", Mme de Staël wrote in 1811, in *De l'Allemagne*, "has brought almost all of them back to feelings of religion." That was the cultural revolution, the "philosophical ferment" which created the setting in which the Church found itself, once freed by the secularization from the *ancien régime*. The Catholic revival was favoured by the romantic movement, but it was enabled to seize its advantage because the sense of the need for reform from within had been inculcated by the Enlightenment.

The Enlightenment in Germany shades off into the romantic period because *Aufklärung* was never more than one element in a varied scene. In France, Enlightenment meant the formidable clique whose battle cry was *écrasez l'infâme*, the heirs of Pierre Bayle, the *philosophes* and *libertins*, the encyclopedists, always talking, writing, quarrelling, brilliant, Deists or rationalists or materialists, with Voltaire for their champion. In Germany, the Enlightenment in that political sense was a novelty imported by Voltaire and Maupertuis, which Goethe, when he visited Berlin, thought frenchified and superficial. Beyond the Rhine the *Aufklärung* was not run by *philosophes*, and by the former pupils of the Jesuits in revolt against their masters, but by men who had studied theology, who read the Bible, by prince-bishops, pedagogues and reforming pastors, by men with a moral purpose whose zeal was not set upon the extermination of the Church but the purification of Christianity. The bent of the German mind towards metaphysics rendered it largely immune to the meretricious arguments of Voltaire's *Dictionnaire philosophique*, and Diderot's *Encyclopédie*. The Germans looked back not to Bayle but to Leibniz, who had corresponded with Bossuet and desired the reunion of the Churches. The Berlin *Aufklärunger*, Mendelssohn and Nicolai, were untypical of the age whose lights were Lessing and Wolff. *Aufklärung* did not mean a rationalistic philosophy so much as a rationalizing reformation. One of its most popular forms was the apologetics of Wolff who defended Lutheranism on grounds, so he claimed, taken from Aquinas. His method was sufficiently elastic to be adopted by some Catholic theologians in preference to the scholasticism of Suarez. The fanatical anti-religious note was rare outside Berlin. The pietist tradition was strong enough to set limits to its spread. Weimar, not Berlin, was the cultural capital.

The characteristic note of the German Enlightenment was its concern with education and its consciousness of the growing importance of the people, a feeling strengthened by the romantic grasp of the *Volk* as a cultural agent, to which Herder first gave currency. Education was the slogan of the moment, and it was not merely popularized in the form of a novel, as in Rousseau's *Émile*; the theories of Lavater, Salzmann, of Pestalozzi and Overberg were put into practice. If Germany was not de-Christianized on the same scale as France, it was in no small degree owing to the emphasis upon education. The age of pedagogy led to the revival of pastoral theology, and the contact between clergy and people was not lost, even if the reforms introduced seemed to the next generation concessions to an irreligious age.

The desire for reform from within was an inalienable heritage in the country of the Reformation. As the Counterreformation, which flowered in the Baroque period, died down it did not become stereotyped, as in France, but remained open to new ideas. The Church, dispersed and decentralized, and its episcopate often disorientated, was infected by the national

movement for good as much as for ill, and without losing it
identity underwent a comparable metamorphosis, shedding
its shell, assimilating and rejecting the thought of the time
as it had always done in its vital periods, and coming to terms
with the situation in which it had to fulfil its mission without
compromising its inheritance. The Catholic historians of the
nineteenth century looked askance at the "reformers" of this
period, but their standards are no longer ours. In retrospect
it can be seen that the concern to rejuvenate Catholicism,
even if it led in some instances to a naïve or exaggerated confidence in the panaceas of the moment, kept the door open. As
a result the generation which followed could profit as the
"revolution", which seemed at first to be leading towards an
undogmatic moralistic religion, proved, in the words of Mme
de Staël, to be leading men's minds back to religion, or as
Rousseau, the prophet of the romantic movement, wrote, to
"the religion of your fathers". The moralism of German Enlightenment debouched in the Christian revival of the following age, of the romantic period.

CHAPTER III

THE ORIGINS OF THE ROMANTIC RENAISSANCE

The romantic movement has always escaped neat definition, not because it was inchoate, but because it was a movement, a development, a turning point in European culture as general and significant as the Renaissance. No one was more alive to its historical importance than Acton, and when he speaks of the romantic movement he can find no better way of conveying its significance than by comparing it with the Renaissance, calling it the romantic renaissance and insisting on its universal character. But with his curious limitations, his inability to perceive the importance of the aesthetic sphere, he saw it mainly as a second, and more fruitful "revival of learning", the re-birth of *Wissenschaft*, and for the same reasons misunderstood the logical sequence by which it grew out of the *Aufklärung*. To Acton "the romantic reaction" began with the invasion of 1794 and was "the revolt of outraged history". But when he begins to think of it as the father of modern history he does justice to his subject.

> Whereas the pagan Renaissance was the artificial resurrection of a world long dead, the romantic Renaissance revived the natural order ... They trifled for a time with fancy, [he writes of the romantics] but they doubled the horizon of Europe. They admitted India to an equality with Greece,

medieval Rome with classical; and the thoughts they set in motion produced Creuzer's comparative Mythology and Bopp's Conjugations, Grimm's enthusiasm for the liberty and belief of Odin's worshippers, and Ottfried Müller's zeal for the factor of race.[1]

But even if Acton's list were completed, and if the seminal ideas of the romantic movement in the fields of psychology, the social sciences, the origins of Christianity, comparative religion, the history of art and literary criticism, were added, it would still be necessary to stress the characteristically synthetic endeavour of its philosophers, the creation of historical theology, and of religious philosophy. What is most striking about the period as a whole is the fact that it doubled the inward as well as the outward horizon of Europe, renewed poetry as well as *Wissenschaft*, drove imagination and "science" hand in hand. Nothing comparable occurred in England or France and the only English romantic, in the full German sense of the term, is Samuel Taylor Coleridge, philosopher, critic, theologian, poet, political writer and autobiographer.

There is of course a formal sense in which the date and place of birth of the romantic renaissance could be given. When Fichte, Schelling, Steffens and the Schlegels gathered in Jena in 1796, Schiller was still living in the university town, Novalis was close by, and Goethe supervised the whole, at a convenient distance, from Weimar. By 1800 internal dissensions had broken up the group, and when it reformed in Berlin it was enriched by Schleiermacher, Tieck and Wackenroder. Towards 1807 Heidelberg became another centre and the names of Brentano, Arnim and Görres must be added to that of Creuzer: Hegel makes his official entry with his *Phenomenologie des Geistes* written in Jena in 1807. He had studied in Tübingen with Schelling and the greatest of the

[1] "German Schools of History" in *Historical Essays and Studies*, p. 346.

romantic poets, Hölderlin, but by 1807 he and Schelling had quarrelled, and Hölderlin's mind had given way. By then the movement was general and its various currents were clearly distinguishable. Schelling was lecturing in Munich, Friedrich Schlegel in Cologne, Savigny in Landshut. Each time the movement erupted in a new place it added a new note to the general harmony: literary romanticism with Tieck and Wackenroder; theology with Schleiermacher, folksongs and mythology with Arnim and Creuzer, the law with Savigny, religious conversion with Friedrich Schlegel and finally the synthesis of Hegel. So broad a movement cannot usefully be described as a "reaction" and, of the contradictory terms used by Acton, renaissance is manifestly the proper description.

Goethe is not without reason the symbol of the German cultural tradition in a sense that could hardly be paralleled among the writers of England or France. Born in 1749 in the heart of Germany, his life-span coincided with the great period of German letters and philosophy, and his work expresses almost every phase in the unfolding of ideas from *Werther* and the *Sturm und Drang*, through the *Römische Elegien* and *Wilhelm Meister* on to the second part of *Faust* and the *West Oestliche Divan*. Nothing could be more misleading than his often quoted description of romanticism as "unhealthy". His whole way of thought, his friendship with Herder, his debt to Hamann, his influence on the Schlegels, and his interest in them, his admiration for Hegel in whom he saw an intellectual brother whose relationship to him was written in the stars— they were born on consecutive days—his feeling for organic historical development, all this suggests how deeply and detachedly he was involved in the movement which embraced the last thirty years of his long life. From the first he had recognized the younger generation as continuing his own discoveries. It would have been more than human not to have responded to the Schlegels who mentioned *Wilhelm*

Meister in the same breath as the French Revolution and Fichte's *Wissenschaftslehre* among the signs of the times.

Friedrich Schlegel, indeed, was the first critic to perceive the revolutionary character of the poetry of the *Roman Elegies*, and proclaimed their author the first modern or romantic poet. Goethe was sufficiently flattered to produce Schlegel's one drama, in Weimar, and had to rise in his seat in the theatre to silence the catcalls. Moreover, it was not Schlegel's personality which attracted him; but though he shared something of Schiller's dislike for the young man, he did his best to keep the peace between them, and pointedly refrained from taking Schiller's side. The other brother, August Wilhelm Schlegel, was altogether smoother, and when his wife Caroline left him for Schelling, Goethe facilitated the divorce, and subsequently recommended Wilhelm as tutor to Mme de Staël. Fichte, in trouble over his supposed atheism, found Goethe sympathetic but powerless; and later, when Hegel found himself with an illegitimate child on his hands, Goethe helped to arrange matters. Goethe certainly felt that the romantic movement was not a reaction against his ideas, but a development with not all of which he could sympathize or agree.

The romantic renaissance, then, was not a reaction against the *Aufklärung*, but a synthesis of the two currents represented by the Pietists and the *Aufklärer*, an attempt to unite mind and heart, rationalism and mysticism, and to escape from the dualism of the past. If the Enlightenment was the age of the balanced antithesis, the romantics preferred the paradox. It is Goethe once again who illustrates the continuity of the whole period. His feeling for the cryptic work of Hamann is the best proof of his agreement with the principal theme of the romantic movement; and in Book XII of *Dichtung und Wahrheit*, where he writes of his intention to edit Hamann's works, he explains the source of his enthusiasm for the most paradoxical of authors.

The principle to which all Hamann's affirmations lead back is this: "Everything a man does, whether in action, work or otherwise, must spring from the united power of all his faculties; everything isolated is to be rejected." A splendid maxim! but not easy to carry out. It is no doubt applicable in life and in art; but when it comes to communication in words, which is not poetic, a great difficulty arises. For the word must detach itself and become isolated in order to say and to mean something. In speaking, a man must for the moment be one-sided; there can be no communication without particularization.

Hamann avoided the "great difficulty" by stating his intuitions and affirmations without bothering to link them together logically. Clarity was the least of his worries. The volcano erupts and the reader is left to make the best of the allusions, symbols and images which fall around him. As Hegel says, "Hamann extends his fist instead of an open hand"; but this did not prevent Hegel from reading him with enthusiasm and writing what is still the best short account of his ideas. The fusion of thought and life might be expressed obscurely, but it never lacked the ring of truth and authority. Hamann was the first romantic thinker and his existential thought was to sound through the works of Fichte, Schelling, Schlegel and Hegel and finally to come to itself in Kierkegaard.[2]

Johann Georg Hamann (1729–86) was too eccentric a figure and his thought was too personal to be easily assimilable. He is the origin and source of romantic existentialism; but his influence was subterranean, intermittent and indirect—until Kierkegaard returned to the fountain head and borrowed from Hegel's dialectic to express Hamann's thought. Herder, his friend and pupil, transmitted part of his message, but in doing so transposed it, simplified it and watered it

[2] Kierkegaard, it is well known, was a great admirer of Hamann. What is not always realized, is that the *Final Postscript* is an attempt to solve the "great difficulty" which Goethe raised with reference to Hamann. The real problem, in Kierkegaard's view, is the problem of communication.

down till the essential Christian note, and the dogmatic core, were lost.

Nevertheless, Hamann may be regarded as the German counterpart to Rousseau—a Rousseau whose religion was Christianity and whose Christianity was dogmatic. His criticism of the Berlin Enlightenment, his influence on Herder, his correspondence with Jacobi, the impressions his ideas made upon Goethe and Hegel, all illustrate as clearly as Rousseau's influence on Kant, the limits beyond which the *Aufklärung* did not extend.

The transition from the *Aufklärung* to the romantic movement and the "philosophical ferment" referred to by Sailer, was inaugurated by Hamann's friend and neighbour in Königsberg, Immanuel Kant. Once Kant's critiques became known the philosophical rationalism of Wolff disappeared without a trace, *spurlos versunken*. The Enlightenment in Germany had always been independent of philosophical rationalism, Kant's work disposed of what was inessential and emphasized the moral and practical aspects of the *Aufklärung*. The opening words of his pamphlet *Was ist Aufklärung?* gave the answer which his compatriots awaited, and defined the intellectual revolution which Mme de Staël could see thirty years later had led to a religious revival.

> Enlightenment [Kant begins] means the emergence of man from a childhood of which he himself is guilty. To be a minor means to be incapable of using one's reason without being directed by another. And Minority is one's own responsibility when it is caused not by lack of understanding, but by the lack of decision and of the courage to act independently. *Sapere aude!* Have the courage to use your understanding, is the motto of the *Aufklärung*.

The motto itself (*sapere aude*) had been used on a medal struck in honour of Leibniz and Wolff. Kant was underlining the character of the German Enlightenment in which the emancipation of thought was always seen as the obverse of moral responsibility, and reflection counter-balanced by the need for decision. The consequence of his critique of pure reason, though it might seem at first to dissociate thought and action, was in practice to stimulate his readers, the young men of the next generation, to look for an escape from his particular dualism, and so to elaborate in one form or another a "philosophy of life", a *Lebensphilosophie*, to recall Schegel's title, so that Hegel himself relished the existentialism of Hamann. It was this dynamic conception of the unity of life and thought which restored the bonds between religion and culture and transformed the Enlightenment from within so that instead of appearing as a reaction, romanticism comes as a renaissance. The static, mechanistic view of the age of reason was replaced by an organic, historic and evolutionary view.

CHAPTER IV

THE CATHOLIC REVIVAL

The older histories of the Catholic Church in Germany, written, like Goyau's, before the history of the romantic movement had been studied in any detail, give an over-simplified account of the inroads of rationalism and of the ultramontane reaction which restored the authority of Rome and a "traditional" theology. Even Goyau's scholarly work—outstanding considering the date at which it was written—fails to bring out the continuity of the life of the Church. Indeed, it would not be too much to say that the history of Catholicism in Germany has followed the history of the romantic movement. At first it was customary to draw a sharp line between the Enlightenment and the romantic "reaction", between Dalberg, Sailer and Wessenberg as belonging to the former, and the Munich of Görres and his circle as "returning" to an ultramontane Catholicism. The picture has undergone a considerable change. Dalberg and Wessenberg are given the benefit of the doubt; Sailer, whom Funk and Eschweiler had revealed as a link between *Aufklärung* and romanticism, appears in Geiselmann's studies as the first of the Catholic romantics.

The breach in the continuity of the German Catholic tradition does not occur at the end of the eighteenth century, but in 1863, and resulted in the *Kulturkampf*; and it ends with the revival which began in the present century, with a return to the ideals of the earlier period.

The note of Catholicism in Germany, except during the *Kulturkampf* period, has always been its intellectual tradition, so that although politically conservative it remained far more progressive in its attitude to social problems than elsewhere. It was never political in the sense which is true of the Church in France because it had never been a State Church. Its habit of mind had been formed in the late eighteenth and early nineteenth century, and that habit of mind, though it underwent great changes, could do so without loss of continuity.

In the decade before the Secularization (1770–1800) the inner life of the Church was safeguarded by two interlocking factors: its very gradual re-integration in the cultural life of the nation after the breakdown of the baroque or counter-reformation movement; and the desire for reform from within. Both factors were favoured by the form which the Enlightenment took in Germany, and furthermore by the desire of the Church and the Churches to make common cause against infidelity. It was not, as Acton says, the romantic movement which "obliterated the distinction of creeds" but the religious movement at the end of the eighteenth century. The controversies came later, as theology revived.

Since the death of the Jesuit poet, Johannes Scheffler, known under the name of Angelus Silesius (1624–77), Catholics had contributed little to the literary life of the country. But after 1770 a change becomes noticeable that can be followed as it works itself out in North and South, in Münster and Bavaria, gradually shaping into the Catholic revival. In both centres the change manifests itself in the first place as a realization that habit and custom could no longer be relied upon, and that in a period of emancipation, personal responsibility throws an altogether new emphasis upon education. The reformers of this period, who laid the foundations for the future, were acutely alive to the cultural inferiority of Catholics. "Are we differently made from our Protestant brothers?" Eulogius Schneider asked in 1789. "Do we breathe a Boethian air while they live under an Attic sky?"[1] And while the Archbishop of Salzburg sent his students to study under Kant in Königsberg, Fürstenberg and Overberg in Münster, Sailer in Dillingen and Landshut, Dalberg in Aschaffenburg and later his coadjutor, Wessenberg in Constance, all pursued broadly the same aim. The crucial problem during the last decades of the eighteenth century was not Febronianism or Josephism, as is often made to appear, but the renewal of the cultural life of the Catholic population and all that that implied for religion. The importance of the work done has slowly come to light as the interest of historians shifted away from the relations of Church and State.

MÜNSTER AND THE PRINCESS GALLITZIN

Franz von Fürstenberg governed Münster as vicar-general for fifty years. Born in 1729 he studied under the Jesuits in Cologne, returning shortly after to Münster. Under his enlightened administration, the suffragan see of Münster, which belonged to Cologne, enjoyed a long period of prosperity, so that when the Freiherr vom Stein visited the province he praised its clergy and its people as a model for Christian Germany. Nowhere else had the welfare of the people been given the same consideration, the schools and hospitals so efficiently organized, and the traditional rôle of the Church in a Catholic community so closely integrated in a changing society. The transition from the eighteenth century to the nineteenth was accomplished under Fürstenberg and the circle of friends with which he associated.

Of these the outstanding figure was Princess Gallitzin. When she first came to Münster in the summer of 1779, accompanied by her two children and the philosopher Hemsterhuys, she was on her way to Switzerland intending to settle in Rousseau's country and devote herself to the educa-

[1] Fr Fuchs in *Widerbegegnung von Kirche und Kultur*, p. 11.

tion of her son and daughter. As lady-in-waiting to the Princess Frederick of Prussia, this daughter of a Prussian Field-Marshal, whose mother was a Catholic, had met and married Prince Gallitzin, the cultural attaché, as we should now say, at the Russian Embassy in Paris. Through Gallitzin, who was then appointed ambassador to The Hague, Amalie met Diderot and charmed him. Encouraged by Diderot, with whom she talked and argued incessantly, and with her husband's full approval, she renounced the world to become a whole-time blue-stocking. Under the guidance of Hemsterhuys, Amalie Gallitzin began her philosophical studies, but his platonic religion, his belief in a "moral sense", and his scholar's predilections, though they freed her from the Deism to which she had been leaning, could not satisfy her ardent mind. Fürstenberg and his work made an immediate impression upon her and she determined then and there to settle in Münster. At first it was agreed that he might not try to "convert" her, and indeed she was destined to convert herself. But inevitably the discussions broke out, and then, as she read and re-read the Scriptures, she found herself obliged to yield inch by inch. In 1786 she was formally reconciled with the Church.

It was Amalie Gallitzin, with her masculine intelligence and her tireless intellectual curiosity, who gave Münster's circle its cachet. As in her relations with Hemsterhuys, the admirer turned the tables on her master and was soon consulted on all matters. Her eccentric charm added lustre to Fürstenberg's kingdom. Friederich Jacobi, "the philosopher of Pemplefort" who defended *les raisons du coeur* against Kant, and corresponded with Hamann, removed his son from the care of the religious poet Matthias Claudius, and although a Lutheran, entrusted him to her care, to be educated with her children. Goethe, at first disconcerted by the blue-stocking element, was won over and would have liked, so he wrote, to enter into correspondence with her and confess the secrets of his soul. No one before or after ever elicited such an offer, and the prudence of Amalie's character is illustrated by her prompt refusal. Wherever she went, in her flowing robes and with her short hair, she overcame the first unfavourable impression and won an unwilling admiration—only Caroline Schlegel remained unimpressed. It was the Münster circle, with its links with the intellectual life of the day, that provided the setting for the first of the conversions that broke the peace, and reminded men of the distinction of creeds, and shocked Goethe. In 1800 his friend, the poet Leopold Graf zu Stolberg, was received into the Church.

But, as in the case of Sailer, the pre-romantic revival of Catholicism was not solely concerned with education and culture. To a degree which is easily overlooked, the spiritual heritage of Catholicism was received back from sources beyond the pale of the Church. For the rationalistic current within the Church was not of purely foreign origin, and the suppression of the contemplative orders by Joseph II was not the main cause of its spiritual aridity. The Jesuits had long since been forbidden to study the German mystics, and the scholastic philosophy fashionable at the time did nothing to make good the lacuna. In the main, the rediscovery of the Catholic spiritual tradition, of the medieval mystics and the great representatives of the tradition in the sixteenth and seventeenth centuries, from St John of the Cross to Fénelon, was due to the Pietists who had kept it alive, to men such as Matthias Claudius who translated Fénelon and dug up Angelus Silesius—and later to the romantics such as Baader and Schlegel. The brief meeting between Hamann and Amalie Gallitzin illustrates the extent to which the inner life of Catholicism—and not its dogmatic framework—had suffered from the emphasis upon the external, the legal, and the objective in reply to the Reformers.

In 1786, Hamann sick and dropsied, left Königsberg with his son to meet his friend Jacobi in the flesh. Stopping in

Münster he found himself so at home in the Fürstenberg circle that he returned later in the summer. He died a few weeks later and was buried in the park of Amalie Gallitzin's house. Neither had been disturbed by the other's eccentricities, and each had felt in the other's debt. To Amalie it seemed as though Hamann had opened the door to a new life. "On that day I felt vividly, though only after a long struggle against Hamann (for she was an inveterate arguer), that my *satisfaction* at my bitter regret over my imperfections and weaknesses was the most dangerous and hidden cranny in which my pride lurked." The moralism which had remained after her conversion, and that was the form which rationalism tended to take among believers, was at last isolated. On his side Hamann had never felt so unconstrained as among his new Catholic friends, in what he calls "that *civitas Dei*". Since his sudden illumination in London in 1759 he had pored over the Bible in German, in Greek and in Hebrew. Now, as he lay dying, he found consolation in the Vulgate, and Sailer's *Gebetbuch* lay on his bed-side table. "I have found delight in my find," he wrote of the Münster circle, "like the shepherd and the widow in the Evangelio."

The reforms introduced by Fürstenberg and Overberg, immediately responsible for the education of the clergy, and their genuine openness of mind, were known throughout Germany. They came near to fulfilling the ideal which failed elsewhere to come to fruition. Dalberg, for example, who has often been singled out as "enlightened" in the pejorative sense, was an admirer of Hemsterhuys and, in his published work, is a minor forerunner of the romantic movement. His religious reforms—as distinct from his politics—were guided by the same ideals, and his *protégé*, Wessenberg, despite his obdurate anti-Romanism, carried on in the same tradition. They were poles apart from the stylized rationalism of the *philosophes* if only through their direct, practical concern for the religious education of clergy and people. Wessenberg's reforms, which included a German *Rituale*, and the use of German in the liturgy, were naturally regarded as anti-Roman. A great deal of what these enlightened men worked for seems no more now than common sense, and if they made mistakes it was not through conventionalism or lack of courage. Through them the idea of reform from within grew and spread, and since it was independent of the politico-ecclesiastical organization of the Church, and sprang from a reviving conception of the religious life, the good they did lived after them. The secularization had thrown Catholicism onto its spiritual and intellectual resources, but it was so placed that it could slip its ties with the *ancien régime* and enter upon a new life in the new world unhindered by the past, less afraid of the future, and more solidly anchored in the present than any other branch of the Church. The belated Josephinism of Montgelas in Bavaria, the Prussian bureaucracy in the Rhineland, the *étatisme* of Württemberg, the total collapse of the ecclesiastical organization in Germany and an interregnum of fifteen to twenty years presented specific problems, often acute. But during those years, from 1780 to 1820, the life of the Church in Germany was reforming, and though what we see of the iceberg is in the main its intellectual and spiritual life, the unseen portions did not melt away: contact with the people was not lost, and the pastoral work of the period bore its fruit.

It is the recognition of this broad picture which has made recent historians more hesitant than formerly to judge the Catholic Enlightenment hastily. Even the much abused Wessenberg may now be given the benefit of the doubt for, as Professor Geiselmann says, only an accurate notion of his view of the Church will enable us to bring that ambivalent figure into focus. For it is above all a new conception of the Church which emerged under the new dispensation, not merely in order to replace the structure and organization which was swept away by the secularization, but as the Catholic vehicle of tradition, life and doctrine. And in that new development Johann Michael Sailer takes pride of place.

JOHANN MICHAEL SAILER

Johann Michael Sailer was born in 1751 and died in 1832,[2] which is to say that he was almost the exact contemporary of Goethe and lived through the great period of German literature and thought. To him, more than to any other man, Catholicism in Germany owes the rejuvenation of its tradition. He was by nature of an eirenic disposition, and it was Sailer, with his calm and his prudence, his openness of mind and unshakeable faith, who held up the ideal for the next generation. He has been called the German Francis de Sales; but if such comparisons are to be made it would be truer to call him the German Fénelon, from whose teaching he derived so much. For in Sailer, too, there is the same liberalism of outlook, the same wide sympathy, the same personal influence, and a poised integrity that won the respect even of those who did not agree with him.

There are other external and precise points of comparison. Sailer was the tutor of the Crown-Prince, afterwards Ludwig I, and if he was not exiled to Landshut, where he lived the last thirty years of his life, he, too, was denounced as a "mystic" and kept a safe distance from the Court and political entanglements. Throughout his life he was in touch with the intellectual movements of the day, corresponding with or visiting Matthias Claudius, Perthes and Lavater, loved by all who knew him—from Savigny to Bettina Brentano—and read as much by Protestants as by Catholics. He was the first Catholic to obtain a general hearing. His influence within the Church

---

[2] Though I have not thought it necessary to supply references in an essay of this kind, I must here make acknowledgment for the whole of this Section to Dr Geiselmann's excellent study. See bibliography.

was no less. It was Sailer who led the way out of the wilderness of the old world and, starting from the renewal of personal religion, prepared the way for a full understanding of the Church. As Professor Geiselmann writes, "it is not to Möhler, or even to Scheeben, but to Johann Michael Sailer that we owe the fact that the theology of the nineteenth century rediscovered the mystical conception of the Church as opposed to the legal conception derived from the controversial theology (of the post-reformation period)".[3] Sailer's feeling for tradition enabled him to distinguish essentials from inessentials and, during a period of accelerated transition, to act as intermediary between the past and the future, between the *Reichskirche* and the Church of the nineteenth century. The unbroken continuity of the life of the Church in Germany owes much to his genius, example and influence and one can follow in his life the successive stages of its metamorphosis.

Sailer was the son of a shoemaker. He was born in Munich and lived all his life in Bavaria, studying in Ingolstadt, teaching in Dillingen and, after 1799, in Landshut until the university was transferred by Ludwig I to Münich, in 1825. But for the suppression of the Jesuits he would have joined the Society, and his early training and his first work, published in 1779, owed much to Benedict Stattler, S.J., the foremost Catholic theologian of the day. From first to last, Sailer was a child of his time, and not of a school. To the end of his days he remained a Febronian in the sense that he had little feeling for close administrative ties with the papacy. Hence the antagonism of the Jesuits of Augsburg, the suspicions of Rome which prevented his appointment as bishop until 1830, and the fact that his first book was put on the Index. Yet at this date his notion of the Church was still that of his master, Stattler. He stresses its legal and visible character, and in general subscribed to the controversial approach already apparent in Bellarmine: a moral and sociological view rather

[3] Geiselmann, p. 248.

than a mystical one. This conception of the Church was in harmony with the religious views of the Enlightenment and was as yet untouched by personal religion; the Church was regarded in the main as an educative society, as a prolongation of "natural religion".

When Sailer left Ingolstadt he broke away from Stattler, from his rationalistic theology and the method of Wolff and Leibniz. It was at Dillingen, in the company of his friends Zimmer and Weber, that his genius broke through. Under the impression made upon him by his discovery of the spiritual writers, he abandoned Latin and began writing in German, publishing the *Prayer Book* that first made him known. His theology from then on ceased to be a purely intellectual exercise, and springs from the heart. Moreover, he broke with the tradition which had been a law of the Medes and Persians, of ignoring the works of Protestants and unbelievers. From then on he and his students read everything—not only Wolff, who had always been excepted, but Lessing, Jacobi, Mendelssohn, Kant and Herder. This did not, at first, commend him to the authorities, but the importance of his innovation cannot be exaggerated. Sailer was the first to break with the Scholasticism of the eighteenth century, with its incapacity to face the problems of the new age, and its artificial manipulation of concepts that divorced it from life. Sailer, however, was not primarily a theologian or a philosopher, but the genuineness of his pastoral mission, so typical of the eighteenth century, forced him little by little to become his own theologian, and his theology was a *Verkündigungs Theologie*, growing out of the situation.

As in the case of the Münster circle, this change of front was due to Sailer's relations with the outside world. Since 1778 he had been in correspondence with Lavater in Zürich, and during the Dillingen period he became acquainted with the works of Suso, Tauler, Eckhart, etc., who, since 1578, had been excluded from the Jesuit curriculum. Fénelon, St John of the Cross and St Teresa were, however, familiar to the Pietists, and it was from this source that Sailer received what he needed. Sailer himself translated the *Imitation*. The change was, moreover, a general one; the spiritual writers of the past were not read in isolation or treated as specialists in devotion and asceticism. Their teaching chimed in with the reaction against the false "intellectualism" and rationalism of the *Aufklärung*, and the new emphasis on life and feeling which marked the "Storm and stress" movement in literature. Sailer, like Hamann himself, was as innocent of the sentimentality of "the beautiful soul" as of the intellectualism of the Enlightenment, or the social and political religion of the Baroque period. Mysticism to Sailer is the form in which the inconceivable in Christianity is grasped. Faith is that experience, the reality of God breaking in upon man, which demands of man an "open" philosophy. He regarded the imagination as the faculty representing reality to us, and making the contemplation of reality possible—in somewhat the same way as Rousseau and Newman. "How should I discover a living faith in the living Christ (in the Scriptures)" Sailer writes, "if the Spirit of God did not send me a Philip to sit with me in the carriage and interpret Isaiah and show me the Lamb that was offered for me."

Sailer's "living Christianity" is the spiritual tradition of the Church, the "living word". The word "living" which recurs again and again in Sailer's pages has its special overtones. It means more particularly the merging of spontaneity and given grace.

The first twenty years of Sailer's active life, down to 1799, when he went to Landshut, follow, roughly speaking, the same curve as was seen in the Münster circle. During those year's he freed himself from the rationalistic scholasticism of Stattler, and through his Protestant connections was brought face to face with the spiritual heritage of Catholicism. Simultaneously he familiarized himself with the critical philosophy of Kant, the work of Hamann and Jacobi, and was thus prepared for the transformation that followed with the romantic movement. Inevitably, Sailer was accused of extreme views, and the injustice of the imputations can to some extent be answered by the fact that he was regarded both as a pseudo-mystic and a follower of Kant. He had, it is true, been in touch with a group of priests in Bavaria (Feneberg, Martin Boos, Gossner, Linde, Siller and others), some of whom left the Church, but there appears to be no evidence that he himself was other than moderate—any more than his interest in Kant could be construed as subjectivism. In retrospect it is evident that Sailer, though in advance of his time, preceded the theologians of the Tübingen school, Möhler in the first place, who were to complete the work he had begun. He could be said to have represented the mind of the Church in Germany during these years, reforming itself and reshaping itself in accordance with the needs of the new world. It was that living sense of tradition, no doubt, which made him a natural leader who, without authority, exerted a lasting influence over the younger generation—men as different as Baader, Alois Gugler, the Swiss theologian, Cardinal Diepenbrock, archbishop of Breslau, the poet Brentano, Ringseiss and Ludwig's minister Schenk.

When Montgelas, Max Joseph's minister, determined in 1799 that Landshut should be the seat of the university, and wished to staff it with enlightened teachers who would train the younger generation of clergy in Josephist doctrines, his first choice fell upon Sailer. The denunciations which had prevented Sailer from being named bishop of Augsburg resulted in his being given what turned out to be the more influential position of professor of moral and pastoral theology. But though not by the severest standards "enlightened", his intellectual integrity and moderation soon made themselves felt. His name became a household word, and many of those who were "returning to ideas of religion" found in him and in his works the counsel they needed. The young Ludwig of Bavaria, and his future doctor, Ringseiss, among the more zealous neo-Catholics of later years, were both his pupils, though Sailer never shared the zeal that was to turn political. There was no foothold in his mind for Ringseiss' Ultramontanism, nor for the future king's "Bavarianism" in religion. So while he was constantly consulted by Ludwig, Schenk and Ringseiss in matters concerning the university, his spiritual heir was not Munich but Tübingen.

Sailer was nearing fifty when he moved to Landshut, but it was during the last thirty years of his life that his influence was greatest upon the young. At his beckoning Diepenbrock left the world, and Brentano returned to the practice of his religion. Much of his charm must have lain in his undiminished curiosity and a marvellous digestion for new ideas. Not the least surprising thing about him was the readiness with which he grasped the significance of the romantic movement, and in particular the effect which its theory of poetry and art was to have. Even before Schlegel's conversion, and before Drey and Möhler began writing, Sailer had interpreted the growth and development of the Church in organic terms. The romantic ideology made the teaching of St Paul clear once again. The visible aspect of the Church, which in his first reaction against the Counter-reformation theories he had left aside, now appear as the expression and working out of its inner life. The static and classical conception of tradition current in the eighteenth century makes way for the romantic notion of the dynamic tradition. "What makes the inner life of a man outward, or expresses that inner life outwardly" he writes in 1809, "is art in the widest sense of the word, and what makes the inner religious life outward is sacred art in the widest sense of the word".

But while open to the importance of the new aesthetic (and consequently to the importance of Schleiermacher), Sailer remained untouched by the new historical school. He was not attracted to Döllinger. Möhler, on the other hand, made a most favourable impression upon him the only time they met. Sailer, in fact, had led the way from the *Aufklärung* to romanticism, from the sterile scholasticism of Stattler to the point at which Möhler would take up the work; and beginning with a renewal of personal religion, and the rediscovery of the mystics, Sailer ended by restoring the idea of the Church as the mystical body. What is remarkable about Sailer is the ease of his intellectual progress, the simplicity of his style, the lack of ostentation. In this he remained the man of the eighteenth century with "a natural skin for his content and depth". There is a style about his writing which the next generation, with the exception of Möhler, though infinitely more gifted, did not possess. He was not weighed down by *Wissenschaft*.

CHAPTER V

THE ROMANTIC INFLUENCE: FRIEDRICH SCHLEGEL

Friedrich Schlegel, in spite of his unaccountable failure to give his ideas the final form with which to bite into the minds of his contemporaries, is nevertheless the most representative figure of the romantic movement in Germany, particularly if, as Eichendorff believed, its underlying impulse was a grasp of the relation between religion and culture only fully realizable in a Catholic context. For this reason he may serve, here, to illustrate the ways by which the previous phase, with its Greuze-like charm and delicate integrity, was enriched and fertilized by the new philosophical and aesthetic ideas, which followed close upon the check administered to the enlightenment by Kant and Hamann. "The romantic world", Hegel writes in his *Aesthetic*,[1] "had only one great mission to fulfil: to extend the dominion of Christianity, and to make the spirit of the Church triumph."

Of the romantics, it was Friedrich Schlegel (1775–1829) who pursued this task most consistently, with integrity and breadth of view. He came of a family of scholarly and literary pastors who had been ennobled in the seventeenth century, and though not such a snob as his brother, August Wilhelm, he derived some satisfaction from belonging to a family which

[1] Quoted by Maurice Martin du Gard in *H. Bremond*, 1927, p. 182.

he soon forgot. Of his eleven brothers and sisters, only August Wilhelm and Charlotte played any part in his life. He had been brought up by his brother Moritz, but the religious traditions of the family, as far as he and August Wilhelm were concerned, had snapped. He came unprejudiced, areligious, amoral into the world, a cold, circumspect and passionate personality, only just held together by a devouring, omniverous, peremptory metaphysical need, by a compulsion that balanced his sloth. There are in fact many traits of mind and character in him which recall Coleridge, that other representative romantic. His idleness took the form of a dispersed industry and the unity and universality which he sought for was too often lost in the sands of his vast knowledge. He began everything and finished nothing. There is hardly an idea in the romantic movement which he did not originate and hardly one which belongs to him. He forestalled Creuzer and Görres in his studies of Greek and Indian myths, he wrote the first modern history of Greek poetry, his aesthetic opened the way to the appreciation of the Middle Ages, he interpreted Goethe to his generation, provided the critical basis for the Boisserées' enthusiasm for the pre-raphaelites and with his brother August, edited the *Athenaeum* where he defined the principles and aims of the romantic movement. His friendships with Novalis and Schleiermacher and Fichte linked together the various strands of the movement—but where the poet, the theologian and the philosopher left finished works, Schlegel did not advance beyond the paradoxes, aphorisms and the brilliant squibs which set off the pyrotechnical display. In spite of his talk of "sym-philosophieren" he lacked all symphonic gift: his lectures, like Coleridge's, are lymphatic.

But where Coleridge's failure seems to have been due to psychological causes and his broken marriage, Schlegel lacked the final grasp and decision which would have enabled him to organize his thought. After sowing his wild oats in Leipzig, he had been saved financially by his brother and morally by

Caroline Boehmer, who was engaged to August Wilhelm. In circumstances which would have wrecked a less deeply rooted character, Caroline gave him back his self-respect and prepared him for the marriage which formed the centre of his life. Always in debt, suffering acutely from the knowledge that the menial tasks later given to him by Metternich were slowly eroding any hope of his mastering his gifts and bringing them to fruition, he was saved by Dorothea Mendelssohn. A daughter of the philosopher, an aunt of the composer, whose son by her first marriage became one of the leading pre-raphaelite painters, Dorothea was a woman of tact, patience and courage. She had left her first husband, the banker Veit, and had gone to live with Schlegel, and had borne with the notorious novel, *Lucinde*, in which he described their love. She has been accused of discouraging Schlegel from publishing and even from writing his mature works on the supposed grounds that she had reservations about his orthodoxy. She may have become something of a *dévote*, but her tolerance was always large and only the blind could fail to see from her letters that she not only made his life bearable but bore the brunt of it. Systematization, and the absence of system were both, Schlegel had written as a young man, equally fatal; perhaps his "failure" should be put down to his lack of a method.

The importance of Schlegel's work, in the present context, is that it illustrates how the romantics, in becoming conscious of the analogy between poetry and prayer, re-established the bonds between religion and culture—at the very time when the classicists in France (Bonald) were engaged in forcibly re-establishing the links between religion and politics, the altar and the throne. In aesthetics, as in other fields, the romantic movement was a conscious return to the primacy of the inner life, regarded not as an end in itself involving a withdrawal into an ivory tower (art for art's sake) but as the spring of action, the source of poetic creation, the realm in which experience becomes conscious. The classicist theory of poetry and art had centred round a false conception of the distinction between content and form, and in the classicist period the imitation of nature had come to mean the imitation of nature as imitated in the classical periods of antiquity and modern times—for example, in Raphael.[2] This emphasis on form occurred simultaneously with a progressive devaluation of the inner life and a suspicion of its inalienable spontaneity which could only be expressed in new forms. Bossuet's protégé, La Bruyère, had summed up the pessimism of the classicist mood when he wrote *Tout est dit, et nous venons trop tard*. The belief in the wholly objective character of form, when allied to an exclusive belief in the virtue of objectivity, had ended by producing a closed world in which no truth could be new and nothing new could be true—a world unaffected by experience, as isolated as the subjective world of the ivory tower. The romantic aesthetic grasped the correspondence between the inner life and experience, calling for an openness to "inspiration" and by analogy to the transcendent. That openness was not purely passive and receptive, but the moment of choice and decision: aesthetic, moral and religious; not an act of the "will" divorced from all the other faculties of man, but a decision, in the sense of Hamann, "springing from the united power of all his faculties". The classicist world, by regarding the inner life as "subjective", failed to see the thread which leads from feeling to action, so that action, instead of being the mode as well as the fruit of experience, had been interpreted as putting (objective, *a priori*) principles into practice. The inadequacy of the view in aesthetics led Schlegel and the romantics to perceive its inadequacy in other spheres. The religious revival was thus implicit in the romantic

[2] The opposition of the romantics to the distinction between content and form in its classicist expression is illustrated by the wholly new importance which they gave to music. To Hegel music is the purest manifestation of inwardness, and the most direct expression of feeling (*Gemüth*): "It has indeed a content, though not in the sense of the plastic arts or poetry."

aesthetic. It was not (at any rate in its best representatives, and at first) a return to the Middle Ages, the discovery of an objective framework for life, an asylum from the modern world, but the rediscovery of the primacy of the inner life.

In an essay written in 1795, Schiller distinguished between naïve and sentimental (that is, reflective) poetry. Schlegel gave the distinction a new turn and made it the starting point of romantic criticism. As in Kant's definition of the *Aufklärung*, the romantic emancipation from the rules of classical art was to begin with a more reflective understanding of the nature and responsibility of poetry. The virtue of Greek poetry lay in the fact that it expressed the "united powers of all man's faculties", or as Schlegel writes, the harmony between reason and feeling. Schlegel was not reacting against Schiller, nor disavowing the classical period. In fact his critical theory resulted from a series of studies of Greek poetry. But he saw that what had formerly been "naïve" and instinctive would from now on have to be conscious and reflective. Form could no longer be regarded as an objective container but as a means of expression, an extension of language capable of conveying what discursive reason by itself could not convey.

The perfection of Greek art, which Winckelmann had rightly celebrated, does not reside in the form achieved, but in the fact that it expressed the naïve harmony of reason and feeling, of the first men in whom that harmony came fully to light. The Greek, as Schlegel writes, is man *par excellence*, spontaneous and articulate, whose work therefore possessed an objective and universal validity. But that balance could not be maintained indefinitely. Reason inevitably and rightly asserts its superiority, and finally in the Alexandrine period does so at the expense of instinct and feeling. The form smothers the content. The difference between the classical periods and the modern is not the aim—the harmony or unity of the faculties—but the fact that it must be achieved consciously: *Sapere aude. Il faut que le coeur seul parle dans l'élégie*, Boileau had written. Romantic or modern poetry must be conscious of its aims; it must not try to repeat the Greek achievement by copying its forms and mistaking them or the forms of any other age for the ideal, but by pursuing the harmony which Hamann preached in his "splendid maxim", the detachment and spontaneity and the form to express them.

The effect of Schlegel's critical theory was to burst open the classical mould in which taste was confined. The eighteenth century had lived in an almost exclusively Greco-Latin museum of taste. Schlegel and his friends "doubled the horizon of Europe", they discovered: the Minnesingers and Dante, Gothic art, the world of Indian myth, Spanish and Portuguese literature. The universal appreciation of art forms in our own time derives from the romantics.

Not the whole horizon could be taken in simultaneously, however, and Schlegel's studies of Greek poetry, which gave him his criterion, led first to the momentous discovery of the Middle Ages. The views already hinted at in Klopstock and Claudius were given substance. The Middle Ages appeared in their totality as an achievement as complete as that of the Greeks, in which the Christian harmony of natural and super-natural had led to the creation of corresponding forms—not only in poetry and architecture, painting and sculpture, but in the social and political spheres. But these, too were naïve, and at first neither Novalis nor Schlegel dreamed of imitating them, any more than of imitating the Greeks. Novalis's essay, *Die Christenheit oder Europa* was not an escape into the past, though its "Catholic" tone and implications were easily inter-preted as such—for which reason Goethe advised against its publication. The political capital to be made out of the Gothic revival was a foreseeable risk, but the impulse of the romantic movement, as of the religious revival, is inverted if the dis-covery of the Middle Ages is taken in any sense as a source: it was at first a by-product and later a cul-de-sac.

"God," Schlegel wrote, at the time when he was defending Fichte against the accusation of atheism which drove him from Jena to Berlin, "God must, in every case, be the fruit of the individual's free activity, he must be an unsought-for result." But in spite of the deep impression which Fichte's personality made upon him, it was Novalis and Schleiermacher who opened Schlegel's mind to religion and to Christianity. When Novalis and Schlegel first met in 1792 towards the end of Schlegel's year in Leipzig, the poet and the critic appeared as a revelation to one another and it would be possible to date the birth of the romantic movement from that moment. To Novalis, Schlegel was the "High Priest of Eleusis" who taught him to eat the fruit of the tree of knowledge; and conversely, Novalis is described in their letters as a Prophet, to whom nature in her goodness had given a home, whereas Schlegel was still "a fugitive, an exile", a Cain who would have to build himself a home "with head and heart". Novalis—Friederich von Hardenberg—was secure in his setting, the most direct and naïve of the romantic poets whose inherited pietism did not cramp his intellectual development, though at first Schlegel was irritated by his "enthusiasm" and his "Herrnhüterei", his pietistic jargon. Nor was Novalis uncritical: Schlegel's essays, he complained, "stimulate and incite without satisfying". But the homogenous quality of Novalis's mind, the pre-established harmony which Schlegel perceived in him, opened his eyes to his own defects: "the original sin of modern education (*Bildung*) is the isolation of man's faculties or powers."[3] Faith in God would be the grace that restores harmony, the fruit at the same time of the individual's free activity, "an unsought-for result".

Schlegel met Schleiermacher in Berlin at the end of 1797. His first intention had been to live in the same house as Fichte, and for a time they took their meals together, but

[3] This was, of course, Hamann's view, but I cannot find that Schlegel had read him.

as soon as he met the young chaplain to the Charité, Schlegel forgot Fichte. Schleiermacher gave him, as perhaps no one else could have done at that moment, a new insight into Christianity. Schleiermacher, like Novalis, had been brought up among the Moravians, but unlike Hardenberg had reacted against this intellectual ethos and though behind Schlegel, as he felt, in general culture, in aesthetic understanding, presented him for the first time with the example of a Christian whose thought was disciplined by classical and modern philosophies. They shared rooms, friends and their thoughts, and began to collaborate on the translation of Plato that Schlegel soon abandoned and never quite forgave Schleiermacher for finishing without him. While Schleiermacher sat at the feet of Henriette Herz, Schlegel fell in love with Dorothea Veit. Schleiermacher not only condoned Schlegel's behaviour in taking Dorothea away from the old banker to whom she had been given by her father Mendelssohn, he wrote a defence of *Lucinde*. Together they waged the last battle against Nicolai, and the belated defenders of the Berlin Enlightenment.

Both August Wilhelm and Friedrich Schlegel were at the turning point in their careers. Matrimonial complications were to banish them from Germany. In 1801 Caroline Schlegel left Wilhelm to marry Schelling; Friedrich and Dorothea had to leave Berlin. Early in 1804, at Goethe's suggestion, Wilhelm became tutor to Mme de Staël's son by Benjamin Constant; the Schlegels went to live in Paris where Friedrich could continue his Sanskrit studies. The move was a decisive one: in Paris he met the Boisserée brothers, young gentlemen of means from Cologne. They engaged him, partly out of charity, to tutor them in the history of European literature—the origin of the lectures published later—and their enthusiasm for the German School of painting, chiming in with his own interests focused Schlegel's interest on Christian Art. When Paris had nothing more to offer, Schlegel, an experienced sponge, followed his benefactors back to Cologne. During the next four years (1804–08) in the Catholic atmosphere of the Rhineland, Schlegel and his wife reached the point at which the final step had to be taken. While completing his book on Sanskrit and Indian mythology, Schlegel had been reading the Fathers and the medieval philosophers. The process which Péguy calls *approfondissement*, rather than conversion, had reached its conclusion. Schlegel (like Péguy) did not have the feeling of turning his back on his intellectual past but of completing the circle of his thought, of making it fully Catholic.

Schlegel never succeeded in giving a wholly satisfactory statement of his intellectual position and he is at his best in the aphorisms of the *Athenaeum* period, and the fragments published by his friend Windischmann. His desire to embrace everything, to include aesthetics, psychology, myth, history and mysticism led him to feel the need of a systematic philosophy, while his point of view rendered it impossible, and what should have become a method, remained "fragments of philosophy". At the same time it is possible to discern the guiding ideas of his work, which make him, rather than Baader or even Görres, the representative figure of the romantic movement as it led into the Catholic renaissance. The notion, derived from his critical work, of the relation between spirit and form and the organic conception of poetic and artistic creation which follows from it, remains at the centre of his thought, and becomes the criterion of his romantic humanism, which in one form or another develops Hamann's already quoted saying that everything a man does must be the expression of his united faculties. It is, moreover, only then that man can escape from a subjective world, that his affirmations have validity, and that he is living in an objective, historical world. It was this passage from aesthetic subjectivism to historical objectivity that Schlegel first showed most clearly, thus preparing the way for the theological school of Tübingen.

When Schlegel went to Vienna in 1808 and entered Metternich's service, the Catholic revival was impoverished. Metternich and Gentz not only failed to use him, except in minor positions where his gifts were wasted, but their *Polizeistaat* hindered him in his work. The Austrian censors, who later refused to allow Möhler's *Einheit der Kirche* to be sold,[4] only grudgingly gave him permission to lecture, adding the rider that no women might attend. His long friendship with St Clement Mary Hoffbauer made him suspect,[5] and in order to earn a living he had to be careful of what he said. His attempts to foster understanding between Catholics and Protestants in his periodical *Concordia* and the liberalism behind his traditional outlook made him useless to Metternich. He was taken on an official visit to Rome, but was refused the post of librarian which he hoped would give him time to work in peace. He was always in debt, his health suffered, and with it his work. He died suddenly on a lecture tour in Dresden at the age of fifty-four. Among the fruits of these last years was the influence which he exerted on the poet Eichendorff and on the eccentric "Baron" d'Eckstein whom in later years Acton was to regard as the one man in France unreservedly worthy of contributing to the *Rambler*.

[4] The difficulty of getting books in Catholic Austria is said to have been the reason why the philosopher Günther accepted the position of censor.

[5] Clement Mary Hoffbauer, the moving spirit of the religious revival in Vienna, was not the sort of Catholic Metternich desired. He would, on the other hand, have admired the type of clergy encouraged by Napoleon and the Concordat.

CHAPTER VI

THE CATHOLIC RENAISSANCE: TÜBINGEN, MUNICH AND MAINZ

TÜBINGEN AND JOHANN ADAM MÖHLER

Swabia boasts of being the rearing ground of poets and philosophers; it might also boast of being the home of a remarkable group of Catholic theologians beginning with Drey, Hirscher, Möhler, Kuhn and Staudenmaier, and extending down to our own day, to Karl Adam, Geiselmann and Hans Küng. When the Catholic faculty of theology was transferred from Ellwangen to Tübingen, in the valley of the Neckar, in 1817, it was already famous in the annals of the romantic movement, and the memory of Schelling, Hölderlin and Hegel was still fresh. It is in Tübingen that the romantic movement had its theological roots, and it was to Tübingen, as far as the Church was concerned, that the ideas of Schelling and Hegel returned to fulfil what seemed to be their original destiny, and fertilize the theological roots from which they sprang.

Tübingen marks a new phase in the Catholic revival: the personal and individual destinies of romantics, the changing groups and circles that had formed in Jena, Berlin and Heidelberg, were to reform in different circumstances and with different aims in Vienna, Tübingen, Munich and Mainz. The religious revival was shaping into a Catholic revival, the spiritual and cultural elements contributing to the rejuvenation of the Church. During the next decade the individual achievements of the past became corporate. In 1819 the *Tübinger Quartalschrift* was founded. In the same year Görres went into exile in Strasbourg and began his return to the Church; Baader's thought assumed a more distinctly theological tone; Hermes published his *Introduction to Theology*; Liebermann, in Mainz, his *Manual*; Schlegel's *Concordia* ran from 1820 to 1823. The first number of *Der Katholik*, the Mainz paper, appeared in 1820 and in the same year Günther began writing in Vienna. These diverse signs, to be followed in 1825 by the foundation of the university in Munich, were all of them part of the process of organization which ended in divisions and clashes as the political situation began to exert its pressure.

But Tübingen became and remained the centre where "the fruitful collaboration between speculation and the positive sciences" was the keynote and remained the ideal, even when the scholastics of Mainz and the historians of Munich proceeded to break the links between philosophy and history. The first number of the *Tübinger Quartalschrift* outlined the situation and defined its aims. No intellectual life was possible without the fermentation of ideas; the theologian must have a general culture; his work must be systematic and conceived as an organism, for Revelation is an organic plan unfolded in history. Tradition is not a fixed code, but a complex living whole. Heresy spells death because it "fixes" one element in isolation from others. It was in Tübingen that Catholic theology rose from the ashes of enlightened indifference and, transcending romantic relativism and aestheticism, attained to a full doctrine of the Church.

The central preoccupation of the Tübingen writers was dictated by the situation. The secularization had abolished the *Reichskirche*, and in doing so left a vacuum that called the very nature of the Church in question; but it had been followed by the rejuvenation of the spiritual life of Catholicism, and the religious inspiration of so much of philosophical Idealism (wherever else it might lead), also flowed back into the Church in such a way that dogma—devalued by the private morality of the Enlightenment—was revealed in the context of Church and tradition. The task before the Tübingen theologians was to rediscover the Church, not politically or legally but theologically, and this they did without sacrificing their catholicity to the fashions of the time, but by drawing on the bold philosophical conceptions of their day.

It was not among Catholics that this labour first aroused opposition, but among Protestants. Möhler, wrote his sharpest critic, Ferdinand Christian Baur, "went further along the path indicated by Schelling, and put the intellectual and scholarly achievements, newly won by German Protestantism, to the service of the Catholic Church". To which Möhler replied that it was Schleiermacher, the second Luther, who was returning to the Catholic ideal. Nor was it only in Tübingen that the romantic philosophies were active in promoting the life of the Church. Schelling and Jacobi were both in Munich, and Schelling who remained there and in Erlangen from 1809 till he went to Berlin in 1841, was as much the liberator of Catholicism as was Bergson in Paris a hundred years later. Görres is unthinkable without him, and it was those who, like Döllinger, always suspected metaphysical speculation and Schelling in particular, who subsequently broke with the Church. But whereas Munich became the home of a political and historical Catholicism (its organ was the well-known *Historisch-politische Blätter*) Tübingen founded and maintained a genuinely theological tradition.

Johann Adam Möhler (1796–1838), the pupil of Sebastian Drey, was the light of the school, neither a dry-as-dust nor an inflated metaphysical balloon, but a scholar and thinker whose unusual personal charm is as evident in his works as in his letters. His appearance in Tübingen may have recalled to an older generation the figure of the young Hölderlin (still living there, in a timeless shadowy world, a *Schattenwelt*) who had seemed to Schelling and Hegel not a poet but Apollo himself. Möhler was the most complete and controlled personality of his generation; and although his work lacks almost all the characteristics which normally go to the making of an enduring *oeuvre* (most of it sprang out of controversies and the rest consisted of occasional articles), he is nevertheless the most living theological writer of his day, and his *Symbolik* one of the few "classical" works of the century—though it, too, is in a sense a "controversial" work: an answer to Hegel's attack on Catholicism.

The theologians of the late eighteenth century had tried to save the crumbling power of the Prince-Bishops by strengthening their authority, but whether this involved opposing Rome or leaning upon it (after the secularization), whether Febronian or Ultramontane, no coherent and valid notion of the Church came into being. Canon law is no surrogate for theology. Nor were the substitutes for theology, gaining currency in France through the work of Bonald, Maistre and Lamennais, of serious interest in Germany. The political and sociological nature of these works was enough to discredit them in the country of Schleiermacher, Marheinecke and Neander. Schleiermacher's fourth *Discourse* (1801), written while he was sharing rooms with Schlegel, and not without reference to Schlegel's aesthetic, had indicated one way in which to avoid a purely legal conception of the Church and to see the relation between the inner life and the outward form. Sebastian Drey had taken a leaf out of Schelling's "Lectures on Academic Method" published in Tübingen in 1803, and had begun the work which Möhler was to finish.

The first step which Möhler took to fit himself for his professorship was a tour of the German universities, Catholic and Protestant—Würzburg, Göttingen, Berlin, Breslau, Vienna, Landshut, among others—but it was not in the Catholic faculties that he found inspiration. Breslau was only interesting as an example of what such a faculty should not be. In Göttingen, on the contrary, he was amazed by Planck's lectures. "Learning", he wrote back to Tübingen from Berlin, "reveals itself here in its proper form: it embraces thought and life. I admired Planck (in Göttingen) but what is Planck compared with Neander." In Berlin he met the two conflicting currents: the romantic school of Schleiermacher and the idealism of Hegel and Marheineke.

Möhler's early work, *Die Einheit in der Kirche* (1825), was written under the influence of Schleiermacher—which resulted a few years later in his being vetoed by the archbishop of Cologne when proposed for the chair of theology in Bonn, on the recommendation of Hermes, whose rationalistic theology was censured a year later. The archbishop, von Spiegel, was still under the spell of the Enlightenment. But while Schleiermacher's notion of the Church as the outward expression of a spiritual Christianity was still running in Möhler's mind, the idea of tradition began to occupy him. For it is as a member of the Church that the individual is spiritually and morally educated. "It is she (the Church) which enters into him, and it is her being and essence which he, in his turn, once again expresses. That is how the true picture of the Church must be given: it is she who describes herself, sets forth her essence." Tradition is "the spiritual life-force which reproduces itself in the Church", "an enduring, living gospel". His argument had been reversed: it is no longer the inward life which is expressed in an abstract idea of the Church, but the objective, historical Church which liberates the spiritual life from its subjective limitations so that it can attain to the objective sphere in action, in fulfilling its mission. In the same way dogma is not the rationalization of pure religious feeling, but the objective revelation which provides the framework for individual life and teaching.

Möhler's analysis of Schleiermacher and Hegel's position illustrates the use to which he put the instruments of thought prepared by them.

> It is generally known that it has become the custom in recent times to derive the religious life as whole and in its widest sense from feeling, but with this distinction, that one school (that is, Schleiermacher) maintains that feeling is and remains the one and only seat of religion, since if it is expressed in thought that is simply for the sake allowing feeling to understand itself; while another school (Hegel) sees in feeling only the lowest step of the religious life and demands that by a progressive and immanent movement it should assume the form of an absolute concept, in which thought, being, subject and object are one.

As long as religion remains the expression of feeling only, it remains the religion of a family or a nation; once it is developed and completed in conceptual language, the religious man steps outside his own subjectivity in order to communicate himself—and it was here that Möhler used the example of Hegel to solve the problem of communication which Hamann had left unsolved.[1]

The importance which Möhler gave to Hegel as he came to prepare his *Symbolik* was not of a purely intellectual order. Hegel was not only the greatest thinker of his day, but had in the interval become the "Prussian philosopher", the official exponent of Prussia's "call" to hegemony. These claims were to be the source of the clash between Church and State that was already grumbling in the Rhineland, and that first broke out in Cologne in 1836. But the political-ecclesiastical quarrel

[1] For a detailed examination of Möhler's debt to Schleiermacher and Hegel see K. Eschweiler: *Johann Adam Möhlers Kirchenbegriff* and Geiselmann: *Die theologisch Anthropologie J. A. Möhlers.*

was ultimately a clash between the Hegelian concept of the relations of Church and State, and the traditions of Catholic Germany. Hegel had from the first dismissed Schleiermacher's subjectivism impatiently (with the famous remark that if a feeling of dependence is the touchstone of Christianity, his dog was the best Christian). But as the patron of Protestantism and the exponent of the ideas of the Reformation, Hegel had no use for a Church independent of the State. The freedom of Protestantism consists in its belonging in the private sphere, but that private religion was at the same time the moral basis of the State which is its public expression. The State was everything. The Catholic Church, on the other hand, was "the religion of *Unfreiheit*, of unfreedom" precisely because the Church claimed, in his view, to rival the State in the objective sphere. The sacrament of the altar, the evangelical counsels, the distinction between clergy and laity, were incompatible with the free morality of the State. Hegel's outspoken attacks on Schleiermacher were now doubled by his attacks on the Catholic conception of the Church. The definition of beliefs brought out the differences; the political implications brought about the clash. And though Möhler repeatedly expressed his appreciation of the Reformers and of the truths they defended, he was nevertheless regarded as a "controversialist" and inevitably so, from his opposition to the official Prussian theology. But it was out of his controversy with Schleiermacher on the one hand, and Hegel on the other, that Möhler, and the Tübingen school, attained to the idea of the Church as Christ living on in history—owing to both opponents the precision instruments, as it were, with which to restore a forgotten tradition and reread the orginal sources.

The importance of Tübingen exceeds the sum of its achievements and lies in the creation of a school which kept the romantic tradition alive. When theology began to revive again, after the long period of quiescence which followed the Syllabus of 1864, it was to that tradition that it returned—not only in Germany but in France.[2]

MUNICH AND GÖRRES

If it were necessary to name the greatest figure in the annals of German Catholicism one could only answer, unfortunately, Görres. He is, as it were, the Victor Hugo of German Catholicism, a figure of more than life-size dimensions, richly endowed and virtuous into the bargain, whom Napoleon in a fit of exasperation called *la cinquième puissance*. He was born in Coblenz in 1773. As a boy he followed events in France with enthusiasm and welcomed the Army of the Republic as an army of liberation. Taking an active part in the reorganization of the Rhineland, he was sent on a mission to Paris in the autumn of 1799, where he arrived to witness the 18 Brumaire, and to be received by General Bonaparte. He had hoped and worked for a Cisrhenan Republic, but would have been prepared to compromise on a loose union with France as a tolerable means of liberating his country.

[2] This was seen as early as 1913 by Edmond Vermeil, in his study of *Jean Adam Möhler et l'école de Tübingen*. His book has been highly praised by one or two English writers on Church history and severely criticized by Funk, Eschweiler and Schnabel. The latter complain, with some justice, that Vermeil does not give an adequate analysis of Tübingen's debt to Schleiermacher, Schelling and Hegel, and resent the thesis that Tübingen was the first "modernist" school. His English critics appear indifferent to the first criticism and to the second. Vermeil's thesis is that the Modernists were continuing the work which had been begun in Tübingen, and in fact that Drey, Möhler, Staudenmaier were Modernists *avant la lettre*. Vermeil was writing before the history of the Modernist period could be seen as a whole; so that he could not see what would prove the main current and what would become backwaters. The parallels which he noted are in fact more extensive and striking if his thesis is reversed and what he would have seen, writing later, is that the real modernists, Blondel, Laberthonière, Bremond (who were not Modernists) were aware of the parallels between their problems and solutions and those of the Tübingen school.

But realizing that France had fallen under a military dictator-
ship and that French rule must temporarily be endured pas-
sively he withdrew from politics. From 1800 to 1813 he threw
himself with the same energy into the intellectual movement
and, after a brief period, when he taught physics in Coblenz,
settled in Heidelberg, where he collaborated with Arnim and
Brentano. During these years he laid the foundations of his
very extensive knowledge and displayed his philosophical
interests in an essay: *Glauben und Wissen* (1804).

In 1813, as the prospect of throwing the Tyrant out of
Germany improved, Görres put his books aside and returned
to politics, and the stirring rhetoric of his articles in *Die
rheinische Merkur* earned him Napoleon's admiration and
displeasure. He had become the spokesman of the nation in
the War of Liberation. Goethe and Napoleon's unrelenting
enemy, Freiherr vom Stein, visited him in Coblenz. Görres
spoke for Germany in the name of freedom, and tepid though
his interest was as yet in religion, for the freedom of the
Church, so recently insulted in the person of Pius VI. But
the kings of Bavaria and Württemberg and the Grand-Duke
of Baden had no intention of letting the liberation of their
kingdoms be confused with liberal aspirations. By the summer
of 1813, the *Merkur* was already forbidden in Southern Germany. Görres' campaign to make Frederick William III im-
plement his promise of a constitution in the Rhineland
offended the Prussians, and when he went on, in 1816, to
criticize the political reaction which followed the Congress
of Vienna, the *Merkur* was suppressed. Görres side-stepped
the prohibition by publishing his thoughts in book form:
Deutschlands künftige Verfassung, with which the Chancellor,
Hardenberg, would have sympathized but for the strength of
the Berlin "system". The murder of Kotzebue in 1818 gave
substance to Görres' contention that only a liberal constitution and a national renewal could avert a revolution. But he
underestimated the lack of political experience and initiative

of his countrymen, and perhaps the strength which Absolutism derived from being dispersed among half a dozen rulers.

In 1819, while visiting a friend, Görres learned that the police State intended prompt action and, to avoid prison, fled to Switzerland where he wrote *Deutschland und die Revolution*. The break-up of the old order, he now announced, was an ineluctable process, a necessity which would allow mankind to rise to a more humane level. And here it can be seen how his political disillusionment qualified his gradual return to Catholicism. The Church whose freedom he had always defended now seemed to him the only power (*sic*) which would survive the revolution. In religious matters, he had come to feel, it was wiser to build one's house in the old building which had been constructed long before the oldest monarchies. This was to become the conventionally romantic view of the Church, and it was in that mood that Görres moved to Strasbourg, where he came under the influence of Räss of Mainz, the editor of *Der Katholik*. His admiration for the unbroken traditions and the historic character of Catholicism is that of Macaulay in the opening of his essay on Ranke's history of the Popes; but the liberalism of his early years was shrinking. The Church was a "power", a bulwark against unconditional revolution, a safeguard for freedom; and in the name of freedom Görres became more conservative. Like so many "middle of the road" figures he did not bother overmuch where the road was leading. He had returned to the Church and he was ready to become its leader and spokesman. It was his—and the Church's—misfortune that the platform offered him was the Munich of Ludwig I.

When Görres descended upon Munich in 1827 he found a ready-made kingdom at his disposal which he accepted and ruled until his death in 1848, imposing himself instinctively and effortlessly by the power of his physical presence and personality no less than by the breadth of his views and knowledge. The motley collection of zealous but inexperienced

Catholic professors, assembled by Ludwig to furnish his university, found in him a natural master. The ambitions of Ludwig I, though never identical with the aims of Görres, presented him with a golden opportunity to recreate for himself, in a Catholic context, the position which he had held in the *Rheinische Merkur*.

At the time of the accession of Ludwig I, in 1825, the Ultramontane party was little more than an energetic group of priests and laymen, many of whom, in the days before the secularization, had opposed the Roman claims in the interests of the freedom of the Church in Germany. The policy of Maximilian and his minister Montgelas and their attempt to extend their control over religion had forced those who defended its interests to alter their tactics and see in Rome the strongest buttress of independence. This situation was complicated by the attitude of Ludwig I who, though rejecting the Josephinism of his father, had no intention of forgoing the advantages of becoming the champion of the Catholic Church in Germany. Sailer's pupil desired a Church which would be an ally, not a servant, neither erastian nor ultramontane, but emotionally and financially near to the monarchy. Munich, as Ludwig conceived it, was to be the counterweight to Berlin, having a university which was Catholic in tone, but where Schelling and Jacobi could find a place, so as to form a pendant to the Berlin of Hegel and Schleiermacher and Marheineke. The spontaneous support of the Church would be more reliable than the contrived Unionskirche forced by Frederick William III upon the Protestants of the North. As the centre of Catholicism Bavaria could more nearly hope to meet the growing power of Prussia. The good of the house of Wittelsbach required an *entente cordiale* with the Church.

This attractive conception was not altogether easy to put into practice. But the hot-house treatment which Ludwig gave to the Catholic revival germinated its feudal sentiments and its latent conservatism. The myth of the Middle Ages began to take effect. A tendency, natural to the German mind, to see politics in historical terms and to prefer theory to practice favoured Ludwig's policy, although this more politically conscious Catholicism had its disadvantages. The controversies which the young Dr Döllinger carried on in *Eos* in answer to the cynical comments of the poet Heine led to disagreeable insinuations. The Round Table over which Görres presided was accused of clericalism, and Heine, who knew the French scene all too intimately, spoke of the group as a German version of the *Congrégation*, the name under which the Catholic secret society (*Les Chevaliers de la Foi*) was known in France. The accusation was unfounded but well-timed. It delighted the Protestants with whom Döllinger was at loggerheads; it irritated the king, who had no wish to see himself compared to Charles X as a monarch run by priests; it annoyed the Catholics who would have liked to exert power from behind the scenes and without responsibility. The episode showed up the weaknesses of a policy which must lead to an alliance between throne and altar and a belief in the ideal of "Christendom". The conservative tendencies of the romantic movement appeared as soon as it became involved in politics, and were in the end to master the liberal elements.

But although the incubation period of conservatism was relatively short, the change which becomes noticeable in the thirties did not lead to political Catholicism in the sense in which the expression can be used of France; political Catholicism in Germany always shared something of the nullity of German political life during the years before 1848, and it was not prejudicial to a continued awareness on the part of clergy and laity that the urgent problems were not political but social. Moreover, though Görres was at his best as a political writer he was not a politician; he took the whole of knowledge for his kingdom and this gave him a largeness of view and a generosity of outlook which is wholly lacking in Bonald or de Maistre. The only writers who merit the name of political Catholics—and even then with reservations—were Adam Müller and Karl Ernst Jarcke, both of whom emigrated to Vienna and worked happily under Metternich. Jarcke was a firm friend of the Munich circle.

The tone of Munich conservatism was qualified by its ready awareness of economic and social problems. It is for this reason that Lamennais and Montalembert kept in touch with Döllinger and the Round Table, and that Baader wrote in *L'Avenir*. The friendly relations established in 1832 when Lamennais visited Munich on his way back from Rome to Paris, were kept alive, and to the end of his life Montalembert corresponded with Döllinger and August Reichesperger. The conservatism of the German Catholics was in fact historical and theoretical rather than political, and Lamennais was not regarded as a revolutionary figure. Baader, for example, advocated the legalizing of trade associations in an article on the "proletariat" written in 1835, the motto of which was: *Fiat justitia et conservatur societas*. The condition of the proletariat, he maintained, like his contemporary Cobbett, was worse than in the Middle Ages and was worsening. The Catholic political writers and economists in Germany had always opposed Adam Smith and the doctrine of *laisser faire*; they favoured a corporate state.

To this Disraelian conservatism, with an easy veneration for the Monarchy and its consciousness of the Two Nations, rich and poor, Görres gave his full adherence. There was in fact no aspect of the romantic movement which Görres did not touch upon and none which he did not adorn with his authority. He was as metaphysical as his friend Schelling, as mystical as Baader, as political as Adam Müller; he wrote on Indian myths like Schlegel, published medieval texts like Arnim and Brentano, and sat at the Round Table with Dr Döllinger, the historian and Phillips the canon lawyer. He was the epitome of his age without being original. Moreover, he lacked what Acton called definiteness and his luxuriant imagery made it seem almost superfluous. Schlegel never found the form into which to put his thought: Görres found it all too easily. With his death the romantic world of Munich —which was not that of Tübingen—fell apart. Conservatism and liberalism, history and theology became more definite, partly through the lack of a coherent and explicit philosophy, partly under the pressure of political circumstances.

The peace was broken in 1836 by the Cologne Affair. The Prussian attempt to legislate for mixed marriages in a country where three-quarters of the population were Catholics hatched out the "religious question". Up till that time the children of mixed marriages had been brought up Catholic or Protestant according to the religion of mother or father, the girls following their mother, the boys their father. The former archbishop of Cologne, Count Spiegel, had accepted this eighteenth century practice without demur. His successor, Count Droste zu Vischering, had been brought up by the Princess Gallitzin in his native Münster, and had not the same relaxed attitude towards the new Prussian bureaucracy. This first trial of strength on the religious question aroused the feeling of Catholics throughout Germany, and they became conscious of the need for solidarity. Droste held out and went to prison. Görres was in his element, and his pamphlet *Athanasius* showed that the *cinquième puissance* had lost none of his verve. It was read all over Germany, and even by Kierkegaard in Copenhagen. This triumphant demonstration of Catholic solidarity in the cause of the "freedom" of the Church drew it more decisively than before into the arena of religion and politics. Controversies which had at first been local became national. The periodicals in which the battles of the Church were to be fought were *Der Katholik* (Mainz) and *Historisch-Politische Blätter* (Munich), an omen for the future when historical and political were to be confounded as frequently as temporal and spiritual.

The Cologne Affair is the moment when Catholics in Germany, becoming conscious of their strength, first sided against Prussia and began to take the idea of a "Greater Germany" seriously. The myth of the Holy Roman Empire of the German Nation was romantically attractive, and provided an emotional escape from the idea of the hegemony of Prussia—without taking into account the character and situation of Austria and its wholly different traditions and interests. The dream of a "greater Germany", in which the Catholics would have a numerical superiority, blinded the "historical-political" Catholics of Munich to political realities, and left them unprepared for the Prussian victory over Austria of 1866. That error, which Ketteler, bishop of Mainz, was one of the few to see and denounce, was demonstrated, as it were, by the character of the rulers involved: Ludwig I's policy led to his abdication in 1848, and soon after Bavaria was ruled by the mad King Ludwig II, while Prussia was governed by Bismarck. The arid temperament of the Emperor Francis Joseph expressed only too clearly the unwillingness and inability of Austria to give the idea of a "greater Germany" even the semblance of reality. "Greater Germany" was the form which the myth of Christendom took in Germany among Catholics.

Möhler had left Tübingen for Munich a year before the Cologne Affair blew up, and at the instigation of Döllinger, was appointed professor of Church history in the university. The Prussian Minister Altenstein had hoped to secure him for Bonn, but Count Spiegel had refused him on the recommendation of Hermes. But Möhler, smarting under the criticisms of his colleague Ferdinand Christian Bauer, was intent upon a change and wrote to Döllinger that he preferred "Catholic beer" to "Prussian wine". He was sharply disillusioned. The ethos of Munich was more painful to him than the open attacks of Bauer.

In the year before he died, Möhler spent some weeks in the

South Tyrol in the hope of improving his declining health. There he found in Beda Weber, a Benedictine, a mind with which he felt in perfect sympathy. After Möhler's death, Weber wrote an account of their conversations which vividly conveys the distance between Tübingen and Munich, between Möhler's way of viewing things and that of the Round Table.

In the scholarly world of Munich [Möhler told Weber] I feel clumsy and useless. I shall always respect men like Döllinger, Lassaulx, Sepp, Moy and the two Görres (father and son) Seyfried, Phillips, etc., but there are times when I find intercourse with them oppressive. I share their clearly marked sense of the Church, but the style in which they declare it, their way of divulging the inner world, and the attitude to the present which characterizes them fatigues me and gets on my nerves. One of my friend Döllinger's witticisms, one of Professor Görres's forceful expressions, an essay by Moy, give me sleepless nights.

This gulf [Beda Weber continues] grew wider as his illness ran its course and the sensitive strings were tautened, which was why he particularly enjoyed the South Tyrol, where at first he never came across the leaders of opposing factions, and could allow the peaceful tendencies of his soul free play; though he perceived quite clearly that these champions of the Church were often obliged to use weapons very different from those which his delicate temperament could bear to use.

This acute sensitivity was allied, in Möhler's spiritual make-up, to a deep seated tendency, namely a sort of revulsion against political writers, who, if only to a limited extent, expressed or defended the opinions of the former *Berliner Wochenblatt*.[3] His opinions in the matter, which he often explained to me were approximately as follows:

[3] The well-known weekly founded by the convert Karl Ernst Jarcke, which ran from 1831 to 1841. Among its collaborators was the Catholic Joseph von Radowitz, the friend of Frederick William IV, and the Protestants L. and E. von Gerlach, and the historian Heinrich Leo.

"Ever since the days of Adam Müller[4] I believed that the Church, as the visible expression of Christ's way of salvation, should be defended on its own grounds and with its own means, and never used or misused as a foil or buttress for political doctrines. Political leaders must fend for themselves and make out as best they can with their Absolutism or Constitutionalism, their Monarchism or Republicanism. It is a poor service to our Church to involve it in struggles in which, as we see every day alas, the political mistakes, all the necessary or unnecessary reaction, and all the sins of misgovernment recoil upon her as the supposed propagator of these doctrines, while the sacred interests of man are forgotten. As a result even the honest champions fall, without noticing it, into the company of those who want to buttress their political wisdom with the prestige of the Church, without genuinely honouring it, or increasing its good name by the holiness of their lives. For being zealous, but without truly Christian feelings, they allow all sorts of expressions, exaggerations and sophistries to creep in, which a Christian filled with the spirit of Jesus and the Church would avoid; and the honest defenders of the truth and the Church have innocently to bear the hatred they excite. If that were all, and only superior minds, though lacking in genuine feeling for the Church, put their talents to that use, one could bear with it. At least we should have occasion to admire their intelligence and courage. But their example is followed by a trail of low journalists which fills one with disgust; people who follow along the same path without morality, without wit and without a vocation, and discharge all their guilt and stupidity upon the Church; men who defend our Church for money and advantage, and use it as a means to their impure ends. I am horrified by the bitterness that flows from their pens, and at the contempt which they arouse in unspoilt minds for us Catholics, by the way they mishandle

[4] The conservative political writer and theocrat, at one time the friend of the dramatist Kleist, and later in the service of Gentz and Metternich. The nearest approximation, in German terms, to de Maistre and Bonald, though more historically minded and influenced in his views by his opposition to Adam Smith. Müller died in 1829.

the faith itself which often has to be racked and strained in order to become a useful servant in their publications. Authors of this kind like to place themselves under the wing of Princes, they like to eat at their tables and talk brilliantly, and unable to deny themselves, want to rule with them—a further ground for contempt of the Church which people are not unwilling to make responsible for the actions of the rulers."

Möhler explained his views to me giving striking examples, though I can only name Lamartine and Lamennais who have unfortunately confirmed his statements only too well. Möhler went with evident reluctance into any society where he feared to find such a mixture of religion and politics; and whenever possible avoided anyone who followed in that direction. With his hypersensitive mind, he interpreted many an innocent publication in that sense, and that was enough to make him withdraw from that field.

To this must be added that with his education which made him a natural enemy of the so-called "Grafenberg cure" in spiritual matters—namely the obstinate contention that certain outward religious practices would cure the evils of the age, just as according to the opinion of small-minded doctors Grafenberg is a cure-all. I realize that at this point I am touching upon the aspect of his mind that means least to our time. [Weber was writing in the forties.] But that is precisely why Möhler's statements are so apposite, and moreover we are all of us obliged, by the Word of God, to try everything and retain only what is good. For example, no one was more genuinely in favour of the Redemptorist missionaries, then appearing for the first time, than Möhler. But when he heard them spoken of in certain quarters as a universal cure against all spiritual faults and defects, he was roused to anger, and in his opinion in the interests of the matter itself and of the Church as well. "There is no better way of completely ruining even the best of things", he said to me, "than by declaring it a cure-all. It is just as when our friend Joseph von Görres wants to make the study of rubrics the most important theological study, a subject he has been working at daily for years. Conceptions such as that are inevitably one-sided and absurd. God alone is absolutely good; the relative good can only be so in special circumstances. To transform the latter into the former, the means into an end, is a sin against God and shows how little humility and love of truth there is in man."

The dangers which Möhler felt acutely in 1836 had been foreseen twenty years earlier by Friedrich Schlegel. In 1816 he had been appointed secretary to the Imperial representative in Frankfort. Two years later in 1818 he was recalled by Metternich as a result of his injudicious intrigues against his chief Wessenberg. The incident is sometimes used to stamp him an ultra, but this is to judge his ultramontanism in the light of subsequent events. Schlegel, like Möhler, was alarmed at the possibility that the Church in Germany would follow the path of the Church in France and attempt to secure its position by political means. When Lamennais first came before the public with his *Essai sur l'Indifférence* Schlegel caught the change in the wind and expressed his fears in a letter to Dorothea, then in Rome.

To come to the point, it is through becoming a party that the French clergy are losing the best part of the influence they might otherwise have. There is no greater desecration of God's matter than to treat it as a party affair. The book you praise so highly I regard as one of the most pernicious and destructive books which have appeared for a long time; and I am busy refuting it. In France the first thing to be done for religion is to bring it into harmony with a truly Christian philosophy; instead of which this man has once again torn open the wound of discord in the bloodiest manner. It is typical of French narrowness—as though Helvetius and Voltaire and Rousseau were the only philosophers, and as though there were no real philosophers, like the Fathers of the Church and the great doctors of the Middle Ages. I grant that his religion is not purely external, and that his intentions are honest and serious; but on the other hand it is not a genuinely inward religion. At bottom it is simply a Catholic form of Judaism; for Judaism is the religion of the law, while Christianity is the religion of love, reconciliation and peace.

Möhler and Schlegel illustrate the attitude of the Catholic romantics, the tradition of Sailer. Their criticisms of political Catholicism are important as showing both its source in France and its gradual permeation of Munich; so that when in 1848 the abdication of Ludwig I, the dispersal of the Round Table and the death of Görres ended the supremacy of Munich in the affairs of Catholicism, the leadership of the Church passed into the hands of Ketteler, bishop of Mainz.

During the next decade or so, until 1863, Munich and Mainz competed for the soul of German Catholicism—but a Munich which had less and less contact with Tübingen and consequently less and less chance of successfully standing up to the policy of Mainz. The strictures of Möhler and Schlegel on the changing ethos of German Catholicism thus provide the light in which to see the contradictory currents within the Church down to the moment when Döllinger found himself driven into open opposition to a policy which had become semi-official.

MAINZ AND KETTELER

Mainz, like the Rhineland, had known the Revolution in action and the old Kurmainz ended abruptly with the arrival of the revolutionary armies. But unlike the rest of Germany it experienced the immediate benefits of Napoleon's Concordat policy. Elsewhere sees remained vacant; but in Mainz religion was re-established, at the First Consul's wish. In this way an Alsatian, Joseph Ludwig Colmar was appointed Bishop, and French ideas found an entry into the Church of Germany.

Colmar, a pupil of the Jesuits, had been among the members of the clergy who refused to sign the Civil Constitution. He and his friend Bruno Liebermann had behaved with exemplary courage during the Terror, living in hiding, saying Mass in secret and devoting themselves to their flock. During the first year of the Consulate, at the time of the attempt on the First Consul's life, both had been suspected of royalist sympathies and imprisoned. Colmar was the first to be released and was shortly after appointed to the see of Mainz with Bonaparte's full approval. His first action was to secure the release of Liebermann whom he called to organize and direct the seminary at Mainz on Tridentine lines. Colmar died in 1816 and the administration of the diocese, which remained vacant for ten years—like so many others in Germany—was placed in the capable hands of Humann, another Alsatian. The two moving figures in the seminary were Räss from Alsace, and Weiss from Lorraine. Räss, founder of *Der Katholik* (1820) subsequently became Bishop of Strasbourg, and exerted a considerable influence over Görres at the time of his conversion. He was like all the Mainz men, narrow in his theological outlook and a notorious denouncer of errors. He was even critical of the *Symbolik*, and was shocked by the way in which Möhler acknowledged his debt to Protestant thinkers. As controversy became more common Räss and *Der Katholik* introduced the controversial manners of the French clergy into Germany, the "exaggerations and sophistries" which pained Möhler, the cantankerous tone that Veuillot brought to perfection.

This group of foreigners, working in the heart of Germany, and on the frontier between North and South, where the politico-religious clash was to be felt most vividly, had brought with them an experience of the Revolution that was purely French. They had seen the Church not only destroyed but persecuted, they had known the Jacobins at work, and their sympathies were with the *ancien régime*, with the monarchy and with Pius VI. A disciplined and heart-felt devotion to the pope was the cornerstone of their policy, and they conceived the Church in the legalistic terms of Joseph de

Maistre and appreciated what he meant when he described the Revolution as satanic. Mainz, as a Catholic centre, was the one spot in which the influence of the romantic movement was solely conservative and political. With the backing of Rome, they played the principal rôle in preparing the alignment of the Church in Germany with the Church in France.

The dissensions in the diocese, which followed the appointment of Vitus Burg as bishop in 1829, did nothing to modify their views. Burg was not unfavourable to the followers of Wessenberg whose determined hold on the see of Constance gave the anti-Roman party a base from which to operate. Soon after Burg's appointment, the government of Hesse-Darmstadt required that the theological seminary should, as in Württemberg, but contrary to the Tridentine decrees, be attached to the state University of Giessen which was as Protestant as Tübingen. Humann, who succeeded Burg in 1833, died in the following year and Leopold Kaiser, the next bishop, allowed the situation to drag on, holding an open-minded view on the advantages offered by Giessen. It was not until Ketteler's appointment in 1848 that the seminary was moved away from Giessen. Ketteler did not trouble to consult Darmstadt and the Government recognized the presence of a strong hand. In the interval, these minor tribulations had fortified the Alsatians in their opinions of the modern world, and *Der Katholik* was flourishing. But there was this difference between France and Germany, that except in Bavaria and Austria, the reigning houses were Protestant. Lamennais' last minute disillusionment with the Bourbons was not repeated. The Catholics consistently opposed the rising tide of liberalism, but their attitude never involved, even in thought, any tie between throne and altar, nor any divorce from the social problems of the industrialized and Catholic lands further down the Rhine. On the contrary, the revolution of 1848 seemed full of promise, and nowhere was the liberal policy of Pius IX welcomed more enthusiastically than in

Mainz. Manning would have felt much sympathy with the aims of *Der Katholik*.

Mainz combined a narrowly scholastic theological view and a close attention to organization and practical issues. And although it did not originate ideas it put them into practice. The original incentive might come from Baader or from Buss in Baden, who proposed the first factory acts in 1837, from Kölping's *Eberfeld Gesellenverein*, or from Pilgram who first saw that the new situation could not be met by charity and welfare alone—but it was Mainz under Ketteler who as it were officially blessed these ventures and gave them official status. Germany was far in advance of France because the proletariat was ripe for organization, and Marxism existed in Germany almost half a century before it became a reality in France during the Dreyfus Affair.

The Freiherr von Ketteler (1811–77) came from the same class and the same country as Fürstenberg, from Westphalia which had passed to Prussia at the secularization. But if the régime had changed the men had not: the Kettelers, and their cousins the Drostes and Gagerns, remained and served in the Prussian administration accepting the Hohenzollern *faute de mieux* and the new Germany with a certain distaste but an unblinkered realism. There was no trace of the emigration mentality or of nostalgia in Ketteler's make-up. With some difficulty he had studied the law, served in the Prussian administration and when he decided to enter holy orders the greatest sacrifice demanded of him, so he afterwards confessed, was to put away his gun. Later, as bishop, his French colleagues found that he recalled the Prussian cavalry officer too vividly. The unction of the French and Italian prelate was entirely wanting.

Ketteler, naturally enough, went to Munich to study for the priesthood, taking his political and social views with him. He was to discover like other men of rather few and very clear ideas, that it was easier to write books than to read them. But the Round Table with Görres presiding was in some respects instructive, and such intellectual baggage as he troubled to acquire derived from this grouping, by now already moving towards its end: some confidently held general views on history, on the parallels between the Reformation and the Revolution, and a practical interest in the social ideas of Baader. Döllinger, under whom he studied can never have had a pupil less apt to being "formed". Yet Ketteler was not narrow, though the limitations of his mind were absolute. He saw no point in "the stiff scholasticism" of Perrone and the Roman school; he admired Möhler's *Symbolik*; thought *Du Pape* inferior to the *Soirées de Saint-Petersbourg*, and liked Klee of Tübingen, Möhler's successor. Fénelon appealed to him in part no doubt because Bossuet's reliance on the king seemed inconceivable to him, and the independence of Fénelon stood out by contrast. There was nothing of the Gallican or of the Ultramontane about Ketteler.

Everything as it entered Ketteler's mind passed through the prism of the Church as he conceived it. His political views ceased to count or rather were interpreted in terms of the Church, the institution, the concrete body of bishops, clergy and laity. The Roman Curia did not figure in his view of things and a nuncio would no doubt have found him categorical and abrupt. He was to oppose the declaration of infallibility as inopportune, in the same way that he would have opposed Roman interference in his diocese. His own undefined infallibility was quite enough, and he probably never realized how much of his authoritarianism he had brought with him into the Church. The vigour with which he tried to discipline his clergy was only checked when he proposed that every one of them should live as regulars under his authority.

The Cologne Affair had suggested some of the possibilities of a clerical career and he admired the way in which his countryman Droste stood up to bureaucrats. When the clash between Catholic and Protestant Cantons ended in the *Sonder-bundskrieg* Ketteler saw another example of the type of manly, militant and perhaps even military Catholicism with which he sympathized. With so many of the attributes of a fighter, a quick eye for the terrain, an inherited sense of command, and boundless courage, Ketteler was inclined to charge. At first he came into frequent conflict with his own clergy and with the government of the grand-duke of Hesse-Darmstadt. In time, as he established his position, his temperament gave him a wide influence over the Church in Germany. After a few years as parish priest he had been selected, at the Frankfort Parliament of 1848, to preach the Lenten sermons in the cathedral. He gave his addresses on "The great social questions of the time". As bishop of Mainz he was centrally placed to exploit the full weight of his confidence and personality.

Ketteler was not a politician but a churchman. The problems which he saw he solved along German lines, with a solid belief in the value of organization. The one passion which he brought with him into the Church, his detestation of "liberalism" in all its theoretical forms, gave him considerable freedom of manoeuvre. He could play off Dalwigk, the Grand Duke's minister against the Left, the working-class against the liberals, and until the Marxian socialists came to complicate the situation he mostly got his own way. The Church under his rule was closely integrated and strongly fortified against the bureaucracy. It is typical of Ketteler's policy that when Ferdinand Lassalle, the raffish socialist whose rapid success infuriated Marx, began to play a part and to organize the workers in the Rhineland, Ketteler was prepared to collaborate with him. Nothing comparable was imaginable in France where bishops had to be royalists, and royalists reactionaries. The work which was being done in Germany had to wait for forty years before Rome recognized it in *Rerum Novarum*.

Even Ketteler's horror of liberalism had limits, and he was dismayed by the publication of the *Syllabus of Errors* in

1864. Whereas in France it was a liberal, Dupanloup, who tried to explain the document away, in Germany it was Ketteler who undertook to trim back the global condemnation of liberalism and of the modern world with which Pius IX answered the appeals of the liberal Catholics. But in spite of Ketteler's efforts the *Syllabus* fixed the label of reaction on the Catholics in Germany and placed them at a disadvantage for the next phase in the rise of Prussia.

The defeat of Austria in 1866 confronted the Church with a dilemma which it had long feared. The quarrel between the Prussian State and the Church had subsided—but the particularists of the South still wished to entangle the Church in their dispute with the Hohenzollerns. Prussia, they could point out, had failed to intervene in Italy, in 1859, to save the States of the Church and had allowed Napoleon III to come forward as their champion. The idea of a Greater Germany in which the influence of "Catholic" Austria would counterbalance Prussia seemed, on paper, attractive. The Prussian victory of 1866 made it seem essential to take a decision. Ketteler was one of the very few Catholics who saw no purpose in antagonizing Prussia and relying on Vienna, in which he rightly placed no confidence whatsoever. *Deutschland nach dem Kriege von 1866* did not achieve its purpose. Except for Peter Reichensperger and Chlodwig zu Hohenlohe-Schillingsfürst the vast majority of Catholics agreed with Cardinal Reisach that if Prussia crossed the Main it would mean war, and a religious war. Ketteler, though ignorant of Bismarck's proposals, favoured a dual monarchy, a North and South Confederation—but the Austro-Prussia war had made this impossible, and Ketteler wished to come to terms with Bismarck. His distrust of liberalism caused him to suspect Vienna of being hopelessly weak, and though he succeeded through Dalwigk in influencing Beust in minor matter, freedom of education was decreed and the Catholics continued to lose ground. Ketteler was dismayed by the *Syllabus* and disappointed by his complete failure to awaken the Catholics from their dream of Greater Germany. While his friends and relations put on the papal uniform and joined the papal army, Ketteler could reflect on the elections of 1866 in Darmstadt. The victory of the old school and the opposition to Prussia encouraged the alliance between the Church and the reactionaries.

At the Vatican Council of 1870 Ketteler once again found himself isolated, and the Catholics whom he had organized and led in the past were now ahead of him in the ardour of their opinions. Nor were his clergy in sympathy with his opposition to the definition of infallibility. His opposition was not so much anti-papal as anti-curial, ecclesiastical but equally theological—influenced no doubt by his dislike of absolutism other than his own, but an expression of his strong sense of the apostolic mission of the episcopate. His feelings were not lessened by his opinion of Italians. When the bench of Bishops met at Fulda in 1870 Ketteler's desire for action had to be restrained, though all but one of the bishops attending agreed in substance with his position. The bishop of Mainz was alone to act. A pronouncement on the forthcoming council printed in Switzerland was impounded in the Papal States, and only released after an interview in which the Pope begged the bishop to reconsider his words on his knees. Neither the plea nor the posture resulted in any change of opinion, and the document was published. But the outcome was not affected. Ketteler's reign had produced among his clergy a subservience to Rome which he had not intended. He had said that the prie-dieu was more important than the folio—as though neither prayer nor theology could be deep enough to meet—and his extrovert activism had permitted and encouraged the growth of an ethos that rejoiced in the *Kulturkampf*, in open conflict with the modern world in which the pope was "the prisoner in the Vatican". Since the Syllabus and the War of 1866

Ketteler had been made aware of aspects of the change which he had not foreseen. The Tübingen school, the tradition of Schlegel and Möhler had been silenced, and the struggle between Mainz and Munich, which had been brought out into the open at the Congress of Munich in 1863, completed the transformation in German Catholicism.

CHAPTER VII

THE MUNICH CONGRESS OF 1863 AND THE SYLLABUS OF 1864

The year 1863 witnessed the last demonstrations of liberal Catholicism. The congresses of Malines and Munich were followed in 1864 by the Syllabus of Errors and the hopes of German, French and English Catholics that a head-on clash between the Church and the modern world might be avoided were dashed. It was in 1863 that *Civiltà cattolica* formulated the famous distinction between the thesis and the hypothesis according to which liberty of conscience and of the press might be considered "appropriate to the special circumstances of such and such peoples", but never as right in principle. This distinction was not only "artificial and misleading" (as Maurice Blondel was to say), it demonstrated the gulf which already existed between a particular abstract thought and historical realities, and announced the opportunism to which the Roman policy was condemned if it was to avoid a complete breach with the State. Behind the "thesis" loomed Christendom, the one and only acceptable situation, in the absence of which it might, in certain cases, be admissible to recognize freedom of conscience.

At the Congress of Malines Montalembert defended liberty

of conscience and deplored the Revocation of the Edict of Nantes. Mgr Pie, bishop of Poitiers, a close friend of Veuillot's, was not content to delate Montalembert to Rome by letter. He sent his vicar-general to re-enforce his demands and to extract, if possible, a public condemnation. Abbé de Briey found Pius IX "very excited against liberty of conscience",[1] but when asked for an authoritative statement the pope remained silent. Montalembert's services to the Church were too great to be overlooked, and instead of a public reprimand he received a private letter from the Cardinal Secretary of State which Dupanloup tried in vain to get modified. Montalembert was reminded that Pius VI had characterized the Edict of Nantes as *plane exitiosum et pestilens*, and that Pius VII and Gregory XVI had confirmed this view. Antonelli might have added that the Revocation had been saluted in Rome by the illumination of St Peter's. It was therefore contrary to sound teaching to deplore the Revocation of the Edict.[2]

While the liberal Catholics of France and Belgium were primarily intent upon the practical and political questions facing the Church in the modern world, the dissensions in Germany turned on the question of the liberty of scientific work. To this end Döllinger and some of his supporters organized a Congress to be held in Munich in September, 1863. Its aims were threefold: to organize regular meetings of German theologians, to strengthen their voice in Church affairs by arriving at some degree of agreement, and to do so with reference to the question of authority and "the freedom of science". It is remarkable that while Montalembert hesitated for some time before accepting the invitation to Malines, Döllinger seems to have had no serious misgivings,

[1] Lecanuet: *Montalembert*, vol. iii, p. 363.
[2] For the details of the Malines Congress see Lecanuet, *Montalembert*, vol. iii, pp. 347 ff. Cardinal Dechamps, one of the three authors of the *de Fide* of 1870, considered that Montalembert's speech merited no censure.

and his disciple Acton describing the opening meeting spoke of "the dawn of a new era".[3] The weakness of the liberal Catholics in France and the strength of the reaction led by Veuillot was never in any doubt; whereas the past history of Catholicism in Germany seemed to suggest that with a little good will the liberal element might consolidate its position. "When the French clergy were the most learned in Europe, this unity and authority of theology was represented by the Sorbonne; and in times not far distant the same prerogative", such was Döllinger's theme according to Acton, "might become the portion of the divines of Germany, if the superiority of their training were not neutralized by their divisions." Only at the end of the article does Acton reveal the facts of a situation to which Döllinger's confidence seems to have blinded him and his friends. "Is there no danger that a crisis may come, when the party (the Mainz conservatives), which at Munich could only muster eight votes out of eighty, will invoke the intervention of Rome against the renewal of conferences which may result in formidable demonstrations against their views?" The figures illustrate the lack of realism which encouraged the Congress to concentrate on the thorniest of subjects: the rights of authority and the rights of "science". Among the intellectuals only eight out of eighty—and a smaller proportion if one counted the absent—would be against the liberals; but this was to weigh rather than to count heads, and to forget the world of Ketteler and the enemies of liberalism. It would certainly not be Mainz that would encourage a German Sorbonne.[4] But Döllinger's error lay not

---

[3] Acton's account of the Munich Congress, reprinted in *Essays on Church and State*, is most instructive, though it is more than usually allusive and assumes a considerable familiarity with the German scene.

[4] The reasonableness of Döllinger's proposal should not be obscured by its impracticability at the time. In a letter to Monsell, dated January 1863, Newman considers the "real grievance" of men like Acton and Simpson to lie precisely in the absence of a Sorbonne. "I suppose in the Middle Ages (which have a manliness and boldness

in proposing something of the order of a Sorbonne, but in the way in which he set about it and the grounds on which he tried to obtain unity. Instead of healing the divisions among German theologians, he ensured the prompt intervention of Rome. Mainz was in fact in the majority, and its influence could only have been countered by Tübingen, which was not represented at the Congress.

The absence of Tübingen was in itself a demonstration that the hoped-for unity would not be reached or even promoted. Hefele was abroad, and Kuhn prudently refused to attend. It seems reasonably certain that Kuhn foresaw Döllinger's endeavour breaking on the quarrel between the scholastics of Mainz and the historians of Munich. Acton's essay on *Döllinger's Historical Work*, written almost thirty years later, reveals the inevitability of the split and moreover the extent of the disagreement between Döllinger and Tübingen. Döllinger had begun his career as an ultramontane and a conservative, and had never, except on a quite superficial level, belonged to the romantic school with which he had grown up. By 1853 this had become clear to him, as a result of his disagreement with Ernst von Lassaulx. He had finally parted company with what little of the romantic philosophy he had

---

of which now there is so great a lack) a question was first debated in a university then in one university against another, or by one Order of friars against another—then perhaps it came before a theological faculty; then it went to the metropolitan; and so by various stages and through many examinations and judgements it came before the Holy See. But now what do the bishops do? All courts are suspended because the whole English-speaking Catholic population all over the world is under Propaganda, an arbitrary, military power ... And who is Propaganda? Virtually one sharp man of business ... a high dignitary indeed, perhaps an archbishop, but after all little more than a clerk, or (according to his name) a secretary, and two or three clerks under him. In this age at least, *Quantula sapientia regimur!*" (Lord Acton's *Correspondence*, p. 37–38.) As a result of what happened since Munich, as a result of the Syllabus and the policy it implied, the notion of a Sorbonne has come to seem almost revolutionary. In justice to Döllinger, his endeavour should be viewed in the light of Newman's letter, and of his ecumenical aims.

assimilated. Schelling had never been sympathetic to him, and as he turned increasingly to "scientific" history he abandoned all pretence to a philosophy. "The restoration of history" Acton writes, following his master, "coincided with the euthanasia of metaphysics". Döllinger, he continues, "thought it was Catholic to take ideas from history, and heresy to take them into it". History pure and undefiled, was the only salvation. Acton then puts his finger on the precise point at which Döllinger not only parted company with Lassaulx, but with Tübingen. "Hegel remained in his eyes the strongest of all the enemies of religion, the guide of Tübingen in its aberrations, the reasoner who made a generation of clever men incapable of facing facts." Whether Döllinger saw his own position quite so clearly in 1863 may be doubted, for he earnestly desired the presence of Kuhn. But in practice he was already committed to excluding Tübingen, and he therefore split the tradition of German theology between the historians and the scholastics. The dilemma, as he framed it, lay between a wholly extrinsic "authority" and "facts" supposed to speak for themselves: an authority such as was desired and invoked by Mainz and, on the other hand, historians like Döllinger and those who left the Church in 1870. The "euthanasia of metaphysics" is a convenient euphemism for the fact that Döllinger and Acton were as incapable as their opponents of conceiving a philosophy of experience, one in which the inner life had any bearing upon "facts". The *Lebensphilosophie* of Schlegel held no interest for minds closed to aesthetics, and irritated by the vague "philosophies of history" which Schlegel had left and which seemed to them to disqualify the thinker.

This over-simplification foredoomed the Congress and prevented Acton and Döllinger from understanding the situation. Two years earlier Döllinger had lectured on the Temporal Power of the Pope, treating it as an isolated problem, as one means of safeguarding the independence of the pope which might be replaced by some other safeguard. It does not appear that either of them realized fully that the temporal power was the last base from which the "thesis" could be unequivocally proclaimed, the last redoubt of Christendom. The Brief from Rome which reached Munich in December 1863 was not altogether unexpected, and efforts were made to counter it. The Syllabus of 1864 with its unrepentant absolutism was a shock and liberal Catholicism was not to recover until after the death of Pius IX. The intransigence of the terms in which the thesis of Christendom was stated was unexampled.

The Munich Congress failed—not because Kuhn and Hefele were absent, but because the point of view and the philosophy for which Tübingen stood was excluded, and because no agreement was possible between the narrow scholasticism of Mainz and the "scientific" history of Döllinger and Acton. Schlegel's plea for "a truly Christian philosophy" was no longer heard and Möhler's theology was not abstract enough for Mainz or scientific enough for Munich. The romantic synthesis was split in two, and in a struggle between authority and science the outcome was in no doubt.[5] The political events which followed in 1870 gave an unexpected practical importance to the result of a theological debate.

[5] The same dilemma lay at the bottom of the Modernist crisis, and it is instructive to follow the way in which Maurice Blondel's "truly Christian philosophy" was caught between the fire of the neo-thomists and the Modernists, between the extrinsicism of the former and the historicism of the latter. Blondel's answer, *Histoire et Dogme*, provided the perspective in which to see the problem before the Congress of 1863 and that could only be resolved on the basis of a philosophy of which Möhler and Schlegel had had a vision, but that had to wait for Blondel to become articulate.

CHAPTER VIII

THE KULTURKAMPF

On his return from Rome in 1871, Ketteler was faced with a revolution. The fruits of 1866 had ripened, and the King of Prussia had made himself Emperor of Germany. At the same time, in the eyes of the world, the Vatican Council seemed to have implemented the ideas set forth in the Syllabus, and the pope to have become an infallible ruler, the autocrat of all the Catholic Churches. The worst fears of both sides seemed to have been fulfilled. The German Catholics saw their dream of a preponderantly Catholic "Greater Germany" shattered by the Prussian hegemony; and Bismarck, like Gladstone in England, saw a political Catholicism doctrinally and politically united in every country in Europe under a single Absolute Monarch. At no moment had the sense of a "split in the tradition of Europe" been more vividly felt. The politico-ecclesiastical struggle which ensued in France and in Germany assumed a pathological aspect. Acton feared for his life while in Rome and, as late as 1896, the Chancellor, Prince Chlodwig zu Hohenlohe-Schillingsfürst, believed that the death of his brother, the cardinal, had been hastened, to say no more, by the Jesuits. Gladstone was deeply perturbed at the thought that the new doctrine would set at nought the declarations made and implied by Catholics at the time of their Emancipation, and believed that the pope could relieve Catholics of their loyalty to queen and country. Acton countered, in a letter to *The Times*, that the rights which Gladstone and others feared were not new but old and had never been rescinded: "a modern pontiff had affirmed . . . that those who questioned or restricted his authority in temporal matters were worse than those who rejected it in spiritual." In France, Gladstone's fears were the basis of the Radicals' policy and Gambetta sailed to power on the emotions aroused by the phrase: *Le Cléricalisme, voilà l'ennemi!* (first heard on the publication of the Syllabus). The *thesis* that Christendom still existed, that the Church was a "power" whose rights and claims were defined and inalienable seemed to have been reasserted in a very positive form by the declaration of the infallibility of the pope. Nor did the words or actions of Pius IX suggest that he was interested in such limiting clauses as liberal theologians might discover in the words, the context and the history of the proclamation. The doctrine of the infallibility of the pope was widely held to imply that the Syllabus of 1864 was the prospectus of Catholicism. It would be difficult to exaggerate the depth of the religious and political passions aroused. In retrospect, it is a nice question which of the channelled convictions was more distantly related to the facts, which *exalté* was further from reality, the clerical or the anti-clerical. By what extraordinary twist of fortune had the "religious question" gathered and festered in Europe until it occupied all minds, distorted political questions and kept social problems at arm's length? The *Kulturkampf* is explicable only if that obsessive, hysterical atmosphere is remembered.

To a number of Catholics the opening of hostilities between Church and State came as a relief, partly no doubt because in taking action the State justified their hatred, and partly because open conflict with the modern liberal world now seemed to them the normal condition of a "militant Church". Professor Moufang of Mainz spoke for many of the readers of *Der Katholik* when he wrote that "his ideal was a bishop in chains", and the young scholar, Ludwig Pastor, noted as much in his diary: "As I read the news of the arrest of Bishop Matthias Eberhard of Trier, a heartfelt *Gott sei dank* unwittingly escaped me."

The realities behind these emotions are pale by comparison. But they provided Bismarck with an opportunity of completing the unification of Germany on his terms. The Catholic party in the North German Confederation formed in 1866 had subsequently broken up, and the elections announced for the autumn of 1871 called for re-organization. In June Malinckrodt and Hüffer had conferred, but although their programme included the defence of Christian marriage and Catholic schools it had been framed in terms which made it reasonable to suppose that the Catholics could collaborate and unite with non-Catholic parties. What later became the Centre Party was not conceived as a Catholic Party, but with the intention of uniting all the elements opposed to the uniformity which Prussia wished to impose on Germany, and the militarism upon which that uniformity was to rest. In the forefront of their programme was the social question, with special reference to the organization of labour. But this attempt to oppose Prussia on a purely political basis involved a confusion of thought that bordered on the disingenuous; for, whatever the claims and the objectives put forward, one thing was clear: the strength of the Centre party would derive from the unity of an embattled Catholicism. Windhorst, who soon emerged as the leader of the Centre, was the enemy of Prussia, not a defender of the faith. He had been in the service of the King of Hanover since 1848, and had not forgiven Bismarck for exiling the Duke of Cumberland and seizing his kingdom. But the more these men asserted the political character of their actions, the more evident it became that they must rely on religion to buttress their politics. Möhler's fears had been realized.

From Bismark's point of view the distinction they made only gave him an opening for laying bare the plot. They might declare themselves anxious to work with the conservative Protestants, but their strength lay in the Catholic vote, sustained by the particularism of the South German States, by the Polish Catholics of Posen, by the French Catholics of the newly incorporated Alsace-Lorraine, and by the fourteen million votes of the "united front" of Catholicism. It was an easy matter for the Chancellor to stamp the Centrum as *Reichsfeindlich*, for these "enemies of the Empire" were not without support abroad. The wars of 1866 and 1870 had both been against "Catholic" powers, and Bismarck could allege the possibility of a holy alliance between France and Austria against Prussian domination: and indeed Dalwigk in Hesse-Darmstadt dreamed of invoking France to counter Prussia. These facts, coloured by the emotions of the moment gave substance to imagined fears. Moreover the political struggle was doubled by a cultural war, a Kulturkampf between the liberal Protestant North and the conservative Catholic South. Had not the Syllabus anathematized the proposition that "The pope should and must reconcile himself and come to terms with progress, liberalism and modern civilization"? The Catholic crusade for the restoration of the Temporal Power, in France and in Germany, was a further ground for asserting the Centre's allegiance to a foreign power and its political unreliability. The war of 1866 against Austria had been preached as a protestant Crusade in Gagern's *Kreuzzeitung*, and Bismarck revived the spirit with which, at moments, he felt instinctively sympathetic. By giving legal support to the Old Catholics who had broken away rather than accept the doctrine of papal infallibility, the chancellor stirred up a religious indignation which demonstrated his thesis.

Bishop Hefele of Rottenburg, according to Acton the most learned Bishop at the Vatican Council and formerly Professor of Theology at Tübingen, was among the few who regretted the opening of hostilities. Eight years later, in 1878, writing to Franz Xaver Kraus, he was still of the opinion that the *Kulturkampf* might have been avoided:

When the May Laws appeared in Prussia, I sent the archbishop of Cologne a detailed exposition of our situation in Württemberg, maintaining that, in the same way, one could have reached a compromise. But the Prussian episcopate and Rome would not hear of a compromise, wanted to maintain the principle, and I became suspect. At that time a compromise would have been possible; now it is far more difficult, and the Church will have to give way far *more* than formerly.

On a superficial view Hefele was, perhaps, mistaken, and it is part of the *fable convenue* that Bismarck had to go to Canossa. Outwardly the Church did not make more concessions, but at the cost of retiring still further behind its bastions. Nevertheless, it was not impossible that a compromise should have been reached, and on one of the occasions when Ketteler and Bismarck met to discuss the situation, Bennigsen, the leader of the Liberal Party, feared that the Chancellor would jettison the liberals to gain the support of the Centre, numerically the most powerful party in Germany. But though Ketteler was not beyond reaching an agreement, which would have confirmed the correctness of his attitude in 1866, the realities of the position were already too clouded by imponderables. With characteristic directness, the bishop asked the chancellor whether he thought a Catholic could be saved. "A Catholic layman certainly," Bismarck replied, "but a cleric is more problematic." Neither question nor answer was wholly serious or wholly frivolous, but conveys the unreal atmosphere in which the religious question was discussed.

The Kulturkampf opened in December 1871 when political abuse of freedom of speech in the pulpit was made punishable by law. The *Kanzel-paragraphen* were proposed by the liberal Catholic Lutz, Bavarian Kultusminister, and opposed by Windhorst and August Reichensperger. The May Laws followed in 1872; Catholic schools were subjected to State inspection, the Jesuits were expelled and the seminaries were placed under State control; theological students were obliged to attend a university. These laws correspond roughly with those brought into force in France in the eighties and the Combes Laws of 1905. But the May Laws were never rigidly enforced and remained on the Statute book until 1918, as though to demonstrate the artificiality of the struggle of which they were the result. For any hint of compromise was regarded on the Catholic side as "disloyalty" and Ketteler himself was not exempt from criticism. In time Rome was to come up against the intransigence it had encouraged. On the death of Pius IX, Leo XIII, his successor, veered towards a policy of understanding with the State, in France and in Germany, but he failed to find support among the Catholic leaders in either country. Going behind the back of Windhorst he tried to reach an agreement with Bismarck, and conceded that the names of the parish clergy should be submitted to the Government before receiving canonical appointment. Windhorst was taken aback by what he considered a betrayal, and when (at Bismarck's suggestion) the pope tried to persuade the Centre Party to vote for the septennial military budget, Windhorst flatly refused, pointing out that the whole credit of the Centre would be ruined if Bismarck chose to divulge the backstairs agreement, and demonstrate the Centre's political dependence upon the Vatican. But the pope was so persuaded of the wisdom of relying upon the Hohenzollerns that he wrote a second time, in 1880, to Windhorst to press his point—with no greater success. In Leo's view the *Kulturkampf* was an error, parallel to that of the Catholics in France, though in view of the fact that Germany was an Empire, more easily corrected. What he desired was a reasonable understanding between Church and State, a liberal interpretation of the *hypothesis* instead of war to the knife. The accession of William II and the dismissal of Bismarck encouraged Leo in his belief that an understanding was possible, and in spite of the opposition of Cardinal Rampolla, secretary of State, he pursued his aim. The depths of the pope's convictions may be seen from the terms in which he received the emperor of Germany in 1903.

> I would add [Leo XIII said, addressing the Emperor] without wishing to flatter you, that only one sovereign has acted as you have thought and done: Charlemagne. He was the great monarch who, so to say, made the civilized world bow to the Cross on behalf of God, a mission with which he had been charged by Leo III. Now, reflecting upon your speech, I dreamed that you, the actual Emperor of Germany, had received from me, Pope Leo XIII, the mission to combat socialistic and atheistic ideas, and to recall Europe to Christianity... I would not only compare you to Charlemagne; you seem also to me to follow the path of your great ancestor Frederic II. In my youth I studied his life assiduously, and greatly admired the verve of his mind, the grandeur of his conceptions, his concern for the religious congregations and his solicitude for his Catholic subjects, for after his conquest of Silesia there were grave fears in those parts that the Catholics would be ill-treated. But nothing of the sort. The King magnanimously guaranteed to Catholics the freedom to practise their religion and cared for their prosperity.[1]

As may be seen from this statement of the Roman policy, Leo XIII and Windhorst were divided on tactics, not upon strategy. Windhorst and the Centre believed that the power of the Catholics in Germany could best be served by withstanding the State; Leo XIII pursued the opposite tactics, and believed in the policy of *ralliement*, in the benefits to be derived from working with the *de facto* Government, even in France, and *a fortiori* in Germany. The choice before the Church was between securing the alliance of William II, with whose help it could fight socialism and atheism, and remaining behind its bastions in the ghetto. Windhorst in Germany and the Royalist party in France opted for the latter.

[1] *Mémoires du Chancelier Prince de Bülow*, Paris 1930, vol. II, pp. 19–20.

The *Kulturkampf* (and the corresponding struggle in France) was the logical conclusion to a policy based on the *thesis*; Napoleon III might momentarily play the part of Charlemagne in order to gain the Catholic vote, and Leo XIII might encourage the hallucinations of William II, but in fact the dream of a new Charlemagne was already a bizarre anachronism. The real importance of the *Kulturkampf* did not, therefore, lie in the duel between Church and State, but in the fact that it promoted still further the ghetto spirit from which it sprang.

CHAPTER IX

THE LAST PHASE, 1890–1918

Up to this point it has been possible to treat the history of the Church in Germany somewhat in isolation. The first phase showed the Catholic and romantic revival; the second its check, and the growth of political Catholicism, down to and including the *Kulturkampf*. During the last phase, the uniformity achieved within the Church was to be transformed into an organic unity. This process can be said to begin about 1890; in Germany with the dismissal of Bismarck, in France with the collapse of the Third Republic revealed in the Boulanger adventure, and within the Church by the episode which ended with the condemnation of Americanism. But this presents a difficulty; the centre of interest and activity shifts to France. For the whole of this last phase Catholicism in Germany is quiescent; the internal revolution which occurred in France was only softly echoed beyond the Rhine. Events in Germany, therefore, are almost without significance unless interpreted in terms of events in France. For this reason it becomes necessary to forgo a detailed, chronological account of events in Germany and to present them summarily against the background of the principal scene of operations which was France.

The last act of the reign of Pius IX began with a double event: the declaration of infallibility, and the loss of the Papal States; on the one hand the affirmation of the spiritual power, on the other the collapse of the temporal power. In terms of foreign policy this meant a state of open conflict between Church and State, more violent in France but better known under the name it received in Germany, the *Kulturkampf*. The limits had been reached: the policy of relying on the "thesis" could not have been carried further, and Leo XIII turned to the "hypothesis". This does not mean that the acts of his pontificate were inconsistent with those of Pius IX. Leo's aim was that of his predecessor: to maintain the claims of the papacy, and if possible to extend its power. The thesis was not for one instant lost to sight, and until the year of his death Leo XIII thought in terms of pope and emperor, of Christendom. But by temperament, training and experience he was a diplomat, and in the place of open conflict he desired not merely co-existence but collaboration as implied by the Concordats. But while his policy of collaboration tended to preserve the peace in Germany, and after the dismissal of Bismarck produced a *modus vivendi* between the Government and the Centre Party, in France it produced the opposite result—which explains the growing disagreement between the pope and his Secretary of State, Rampolla, as Leo came more and more to make an understanding with the central powers the pivot of his policy. The effect of the pope's consistency was to stabilize the religious position in Germany, and to inflame the "religious question" in France. This accounts, in a large measure, for the fact that the religious "crisis" broke in France and was delayed another quarter of a century in Germany.

FRANCE

Immediately on his accession Leo XIII had despatched Mgr Czacki to Paris with instructions to bring about an understanding between Church and State, between the Catholic party and the Third Republic, then three years old. This policy he pursued resolutely to the end, and in spite of re-peated failures. For neither the Royalist party nor the anti-clerical Radicals were prepared to compromise, and Jules Ferry was not behind Bismarck in his determination to bring the Catholic party to heel. Leo's object was to create, in France, a Catholic party powerful by reason of its moderation and its unity, a party comparable to the Centre Party. This aim took no account of the historical background, of the intransigence of the Catholics, of the strength of anti-cleri-calism, nor of the theory behind the papal policy. Instead of achieving unity, peace and moderation, Leo unwittingly divided French Catholics and encouraged both the Right and the Left to adopt more extreme views. The net result of the *ralliement* was not to rally Catholics into a party working within the framework of the Republic, but to encourage the formation of two irreconcilable Catholic groups. Out of this division came the "crisis" which broke under his successor, Pius X, but not before the character of both sides had changed fundamentally.

For reasons which it is unnecessary to consider here, the old Royalist party which had suffered a series of defeats since 1870, was rejuvenated during the nineties and transformed into an ideological party, the *Action française*, led by the atheist Charles Maurras, and supported by the higher clergy. The *Action française*, which accepted the Syllabus of 1864, was the logical outcome of political Catholicism; it was the champion of the Church against the Third Republic, and in the eyes of the majority it was the "Catholic party". During the last few years of the reign of Leo XIII it vigorously opposed the *ralliement*; under Pius X it came back into favour, and its leader Maurras was described by the pope as "a great defender of the faith".

The pontificate of Leo XIII had, however, done much to encourage those who were to become the opponents of the *Action française*. His desire for an influential Catholic party, participating in the life of the nation and collaborating with the Third Republic, was liberal in its effects. The intellectual revival, which may be dated from the foundation of the Catholic universities in 1875, and the mild encouragement given to the Catholic social movement, not only strengthened the liberal element which had till then lived under a cloud, but ended by fostering a new spirit. For in the situation as it now existed, it was becoming increasingly clear that the choice was no longer between conservative and liberal Catholicism, but between accepting the situation and rejecting it—between opposing it (on the grounds of the thesis, or hypothesis) or accepting it: between political Catholicism and religious Catholicism. It was of this conflict, with its long back history that Blondel wrote:

> One cannot really conceal the fact from oneself, every day the conflict reveals itself as more acute and more general, between tendencies which in every order, the social, political and philosophical, set Catholics one against another. One might almost say that there are now, particularly in France, two entirely incompatible Catholic mentalities. And that is manifestly abnormal, for there cannot be two Catholicisms.[1]

Elsewhere, in reply to a questionnaire sent out by the *Mercure de France* in 1907, Blondel defined the importance of the crisis:

> The present crisis, unprecedented perhaps in depth and extent—for it is at the same time scientific, metaphysical, moral, social and political—is not a "dissolution" (for the spirit of faith does not die), nor even an "evolution" (for the spirit of faith does not change), it is a *purification* of the religious sense, and an *integration* of Catholic truth.[2]

[1] *Histoire et Dogme*, p. 150, in *Les premiers écrits de Maurice Blondel*, vol. I. *Lettre sur les exigences de la Pensée contemporaine* and *Histoire et Dogme*, Presses Universitaires de France.

[2] *Mercure de France*, April 1907. For a summary of Blondel's view of the crisis and of the conflict between the two tendencies, I would refer the reader to my article "The *Action française* and the Origins of the Second Vatican Council" in *The Downside Review*, July 1963.

For the first time the seriousness of the position in which the Church found itself was being taken seriously. In the place of the customary lamentations about "the evils of the age", which placed the whole responsibility for the decline of religion and the dechristianization of France on the Revolution and its consequences, on the Freemasons and the Republic, the grave weaknesses within the Church were taken into account and the salutary principle of self-criticism was applied by a few. Moreover this was done, not from a political point of view, and in pursuance of immediate political results, but from religious motives. What followed was not a change of policy, but a revolution, which has little to do with the "liberal Catholicism" of Lamennais, Lacordaire and Montalembert. Furthermore, it was not conducted by politicians, or by men interested in the main in social and political questions, but by philosophers and poets, by historians and men of letters. What now emerged in France was a movement which recognized its affinities with the romantic movement in the Church in Germany, which understood that the Church could no longer live and function in a framework defined in terms of Church and State, and that the individual could only be reached through the cultural sphere. And in this sphere, as the philosopher of the movement, Maurice Blondel wrote, "Nothing had been done since the musical prelude of Chateaubriand: we in France and in the Catholic countries have assisted for centuries at the strange spectacle of the whole duty of man (*le tout de l'homme*) divorced from honest scholarship, genuine art and living thought".

This was the real, cultural background to the failures of the nineteenth century, which self-criticism revealed. Since the seventeenth century the Church in France had relied on political power and influence, wherever possible silencing opposition, and finally isolating itself from the nation. Blondel was writing in 1896. Twenty-five years later, in 1921, Paul Claudel diagnosed the causes of failure in almost the same terms:

It is because it despised a part of God's work, the noble faculties of imagination and sensibility (that is, the cultural sphere) to which certain lunatics would like to have added reason itself, that religion has been through the long crisis from which it has hardly begun to emerge. This crisis, which reached its culminating point in the nineteenth century, was not in the main a crisis of the intelligence . . . I would prefer to call it the tragedy of a starved imagination.

(Positions et Propositions, p. 209)

Both Blondel and Claudel give the same account of the origins of the crisis—independently confirmed in the same years by Henri Bremond in his *Literary History of Religious Thought in France, from the XVIIth century*. Since the end of the seventeenth century Catholicism had abandoned the cultural sphere for the political in which it was possible for a time to maintain the "thesis" that Christendom still existed, and consequently it had ceased to be a missionary Church inside Europe, hoping to preserve a static position, its "power", by making Concordats the basis of its policy. The transformation had been gradual, the deteriorization at times imperceptible.

In the final metamorphosis, an exclusive preoccupation with doctrinal intransigence is imperceptibly transformed into a sole concern for the triumph of an authoritarianism of the most realistic kind; this is a return to the *old man* who, under pretext of thinking exclusively about religion, no longer acts except politically, under the august mantle of Christ.[3]

[3] This and the following quotations are taken from *La Semaine Sociale de Bordeaux*, which appeared in 1909 and 1910 in *Annales de Philosophie chrétienne*. Blondel's articles have not been reissued, except as an off-print. They constitute the one complete and fundamental criticism of political Catholicism, written from a philosophical point of view. They were written in answer to the *Action française*, but cover a far wider ground than the title suggests. The fact that they were published under the pseudonym *Testis* is one reason why they have been ignored.

This attitude cut the Church off and isolated it, and its authoritarianism became a sort of caricature of spiritual authority. "Once upon a time", Blondel writes, "the Saviour left the ninety-nine faithful sheep in order to find the one that was lost. There are some, today, who would like to remain behind with the one remaining faithful sheep to secure it more firmly still." And because there was no attempt to bridge the gulf and preach to the unconverted, but only a strong desire to bring them to Canossa, "the Church's political authority has aroused against the Church a growing movement of disaffection and revolt of which nothing in the past can convey any conception".

The "crisis" of which Blondel wrote was caused by the unavoidable reversal of the Roman policy, necessitated by the situation which could now no longer be denied. This reversal was finally and officially proclaimed by the Lateran Treaty, signed with the Italian State, and by the condemnation of political Catholicism under the name of the *Action française* in 1926. The aims set before the present Council by John XXIII are those which emerge naturally in the new situation: both *ecumenism* and *aggiornamento* imply the abandonment of power politics in favour of a purely religious policy.

It is often implied or asserted that the "crisis" which began in 1890 and exploded during the pontificate of Pius X centred on the Modernist controversy. That was no doubt the impression given at the time, and moreover it suited the *Action française* and its supporters in France and in Rome (of whom Cardinal Merry del Val was the most important) to make the problems raised by the Modernists the central questions. This distracted attention from the political issues, and moreover it made it possible to stamp any form of opposition to political Catholicism as "Modernism". But in retrospect (and without for a moment minimizing the importance of Modernism) Claudel's diagnosis points to the central issue: the crisis was the "tragedy of a starved imagination"—or, in Blondel's terms, the tragedy of the "whole man" *le tout de l'homme,* cut off from the cultural sphere. It is of course possible to write the history of the period in negative terms, to group events and interpret them as a series of heretical movements— in the social sphere the *Sillon* condemned in 1909; in the theological sphere Modernism, condemned in 1907; in the philosophical sphere Laberthonière's condemnation in 1913. And this has been done so effectively that the real leaders of the Catholic Renaissance, the creative writers and thinkers and historians have been ignored or treated in isolation. But if instead of rehearsing the mistakes or possible mistakes which were made, the positive achievement of the period is taken as the criterion, the work of Blondel, Péguy, Bremond, Claudel and others stands out in its real proportions. It then becomes possible to see that Claudel was right in saying that the "crisis" had culminated in the nineteenth century, and that the "crisis" which occurred during the reign of Pius X was in fact the first stage of its *dénouement.*

GERMANY

There had always been an élite which saw the dangers of political Catholicism—men such as Schlegel and Möhler—but they had been powerless to prevent its rise. The political character of the century, the attractions of power, the links with the monarchy in Bavaria and, last but not least, the policy of Rome, gradually obscured the ideals of Sailer, and brought Mainz to the fore. The revolution of 1848, coinciding with the death of Görres, wrote *finis,* for the time being, to the romantic movement within the Church. By 1850 Martin Deutinger, the last of the romantic philosophers, was speaking of the dangers of living "as in a beleaguered city", and the poet Eichendorff, who died in 1857, warned his correligionists "not to starve themselves to death behind the bulwarks of outworn formulae". The situation which had existed "for centuries" in France and the Catholic or Latin countries was recreated in Germany. The historian Franz Schnabel, in the fourth volume of his *Deutsche Geschichte*, diagnoses the process by which this change had come about in terms which confirm the prognosis of Deutinger and Eichendorff:

> From the 'forties to the 'sixties, the system of suspicions, intrigues and secret dealings flourished, and brought tragedy into the life of many a sensitive and believing theologian ... By concentrating the whole of the Church's culture on the old and tried base of scholasticism and centralization, the riches handed down by the romantic movement had to make way for a more rigid uniformity.[4]

The formation of the Ghetto was achieved by politicizing Catholicism:

> The ideal of a pure Church was rarely represented by believing Catholics. In Italy Rosmini spoke in this sense; in England Cardinal Newman; and in Germany towards the end of the century Franz Xaver Kraus. These men were deeply religious and learned theologians; they opposed "religious" to political Catholicism and invoked the name of Dante, who had lamented the worldliness of religion and the sins of an external and political Church in imperishable rhyme. The nineteenth century, after a beginning full of promise, which we have described, in fact gave up any attempt to bring the religious spirit of its great individuals to the fore.[5]

The Ghetto was in existence, and the question which faced the Church during the last phase of the nineteenth century was to extricate itself from the *impasse* into which political Catholicism had led, and to rediscover "religious" Catholicism.

[4] *Deutsche Geschichte im neunzehnten Jahrhundert*, vol. IV, p. 259.
[5] *Ibid.*

As long as the *Kulturkampf* lasted, as long as it was an open conflict with the State, the weaknesses of Catholicism could be overlooked. The uniformity which had been established, the authoritarianism of the Catholic régime, were seen as the sources of an unsuspected strength, and the creation of a powerful Centre Party seemed justified by events. But by 1890, the Centre Party was no longer called upon to lead its troops into battle but to assume its responsibility as one of the great parties within the State. This it failed and continued to fail to do; lack of vision and imagination could not be made good by astute manoeuvring towards practical objectives. Moreover, in times of peace, the responsibility which the Centre Party bore demanded not only success at the polls, but a sufficiency of men capable of taking part in the life of the country. The catastrophic decline in the educational and cultural level of Catholics now made this impossible.

Since the death of Eichendorff Catholics had renounced their place on Parnassus, and the national position which Catholic men of letters had occupied during the Romantic revival was forfeit. Poetry was once again a foreign dialect— though it was no longer Protestant—and the air of the ghetto was Boeotian. Catholics, it could be said, neither read nor wrote. Even the classical period of German literature was frowned upon as pagan, immoral and irreligious. The gap was filled with "religious" novels and pious verse. The tradition of scholarship had survived another twenty-five years, but after 1870—when the Old Catholics, Döllinger and his supporters, left the Church—the men who remained were without influence on the tone of Catholicism, indifferent to or conniving at the policy of Rome, even when like Scheeben, the greatest theologian of the period, they were in fundamental disagreement with the narrow and mechanical scholasticism of the Roman theologians such as Kleutgen. Not only were Catholics barely represented in the university world; they were no longer found in the higher branches of the civil service. As statistics showed, the fall in the level of education was no less apparent in the high schools—the Realschule and the Gymnasium.

All these facts and their implications were pointed out in a speech by George von Hertling to the Görresgesellschaft in the year 1896—usually taken as the turning point, as the beginning of the movement for reform. As president of the Görres Society and professor of philosophy in Munich, von Hertling spoke with authority. The future prime minister of Bavaria, and chancellor of the Reich, did not mince his words, and his accusation of moral irresponsibility caused a *furore*. Von Hertling was not the first to draw attention to the lamentable state of affairs, but the first to do so effectively. But although the matter was thrown open to discussion, circumstances militated against action, and while in France the controversy led into a crisis, in Germany it remained a discussion conducted by intellectuals and with little noticeable effect on the ethos of Catholicism.

The chief reason for the state of apathy has already been mentioned. The aim of Leo XIII was not to stimulate a spiritual revival, but to take advantage of the strong position of the Centre Party in the country and to obtain satisfactory terms, so that the Church could continue to function as a power within the Reich. Whereas in France this policy encouraged the movement for reform, in Germany it stabilized the position, and gave the Centre Party a sort of official standing. Moreover, the German ghetto was in certain essentials unlike the *émigration intérieure* in France: it was not politically reactionary, it was not in principle a Catholic party, but had been conceived with the idea of collaborating with other Christian parties, and it was not indifferent to social questions. Its political moderation made it impervious to criticism. And it stood, in a very real sense, for power, Again, however real and alarming the drop in the cultural level, the fact that it was of recent date made it appear less fundamental. In France, where the situation had lasted for "centuries", it could not be attributed to temporary causes. In Germany there was little disposition to regard the intellectual failure as deep-seated and still less to attribute it to a mistaken religious policy. Furthermore the prosperity, security and complacency of the Wilhelmine period encouraged the impassive conservatism of the ghetto. Both internal and external factors muted the calls for reform or made them sound alarmist and extremist. It was not until the social and political revolution of 1918 that the atmosphere in Germany really began to change; not until the central European monarchies and Holy Russia had ceased to exist—the last remnants of the paste-board scenery of "Christendom". In the intervening decades the ghetto held, and little more than preparatory work was done.

Perhaps the clearest indication of the impotence of Catholicism during this period is its failure to produce leaders. Neither clergy nor laity could summon up the energy needed to give a lead, morally, intellectually and spiritually. The authoritarian régime had killed initiative, spontaneity, and independence. In this dispiriting world the name of Franz Xaver Kraus (1840–1901) stands out, and for this reason he has always been looked upon as the father of *Reformkatholizismus*, and of the movement to break out of the ghetto. Schnabel is no doubt right when he says that it was Kraus who opposed political Catholicism with "religious Catholicism", but Kraus had neither the talents nor the character required of a leader. He was the herald, not the hero of the movement; and though he felt the oppressive atmosphere acutely it was only at the very end of his life that he attained to a sufficiently clear view of his task. His hatred of the Curia and of the Centre, the two bases of political Catholicism, had always prevented him from formulating any positive doctrine; his vanity, snobbery and passion for intrigue led him to think that criticism and opposition alone were sufficient, and to neglect the task of securing the foundations. As a young man he had been a friend of the liberal Catholics, had known Acton, Dupanloup, and Döllinger, and remained a close friend of Lady Blennerhasset. Later he ingratiated himself in the favour of the Grand-Duke of Baden, and acted on behalf of the Chancellor, Hohenlohe. This made the historian Janssen speak of him as playing with any group that was opposed to Rome and to the Centre; and it ended by diminishing his prestige, and his influence. Yet when all this is said—and the eternal self-reproaches of his *Diaries* make no secret of his tortured personality and personal inadequacy—Kraus showed both vision and a degree of civic courage that was rare among clergy and laity.

The would-be politician was a pathetic figure; the writer, on the other hand, was gifted and effective. Kraus combined scholarship and imagination as had not been done since the romantic period. His histories of Christian archaeology (inspired by his friend de Rossi) and of Christian art from its beginnings to the Renaissance were a landmark. He not only abandoned the Church–State framework, in which the liberal Catholics had become imprisoned, and revived the history of art, which had fallen into neglect among Catholics since the days of Schlegel, but was widely known as an essayist, and in his *Spectator Letters* showed his talents as a pamphleteer, until ordered by ecclesiastical authority to bring his *Letters* to a close.

There had always been two sides to Kraus. He was torn between his ambition to cut a figure in the great world, and his vocation as priest and scholar—and in his *Diaries* it is possible to see how the old liberalism of Acton and Döllinger was gradually transformed into the new "religious" Catholicism with its roots in the romantic movement. The shift in his opinions, which occurred during the last decade of his life, was occasioned by his meeting in Rome with Mgr O'Connell, and his increasing dissatisfaction with the state of affairs in Germany led him to look for salvation elsewhere, to the movement taking shape in France, of which he was fully informed, both in regard to its purely scholarly achievements, such as the epoch-making work of Duchesne or, in its more general aspect, as signalized by the articles of Brunetière. In a more than usually despondent mood—after Mgr O'Connell and the Abbé Félix Klein had visited him in Freiburg—he notes in his *Diaries* that O'Connell foresaw another "Syllabus" which, Kraus writes, would have been *l'extrème onction*; but the very gravity of the position, the impossibility of going further in the same direction, would then release his hopes, and he would transcribe parts of Brunetière's latest article in the *Revue des Deux Mondes*: "Religion, imprisoned in the old political edifice—the veritable dungeon of the Church—will not recover its ascendance except by recovering its liberty . . . As for me, I am profoundly convinced of the universal transformation of society under the action of Catholicism." (March 1893.)

In his last work, the posthumously published study of Cavour, Kraus took the side of the Italian leader, convinced that the seizure of the Papal States and the occupation of Rome was the necessary prelude to a realistic policy, and that the Temporal Power had become the chief obstacle to the emergence of "religious" Catholicism. He had lost his faith in political intrigue, and reaffirmed the hopes of Brunetière: "The idea of religious Catholicism, once it emerges, will run its victorious course and in a few decades conquer the world; it will build Christianity a new home."

But neither Kraus nor those who came after him was able to disturb the complacency of the ghetto; for, as Kierkegaard had noted in similar circumstance, "mediocrity is never so dangerous as when disguised as 'sincerity'". In the place of the sharp intellectual contours of Charles Maurras, there was the impassive conservatism and rigid ultramontanism of Ludwig von Pastor.

Ludwig von Pastor (1852–1928) the historian of the popes, is the representative figure of pre-war Catholicism in Germany, the embodiment of the ghetto. In spite of his considerable talents as a research worker, his inexhaustible industry, and the protection of his master, Janssen, Pastor found himself, on completing his studies, virtually excluded from the German universities—as much by prejudice as on account of his aggressively defensive attitude. He was obliged therefore to expatriate himself to Austria, and failing Vienna—where his ultramontanism was unwelcome—he became professor of history in Innsbruck. There could be no better example of the consequences of the *Kulturkampf*. Pastor's good fortune lay in being the first scholar to be allowed to work in the Vatican archives and this gave him an immense advantage over his rivals. But although he collected, ordered and published the results of his labours, he lived and worked in exile, uninfluenced by the work of his contemporaries, and with a total disregard for contemporary problems. He had conceived his history of the popes in answer to Ranke, and it never occurred to him that the papacy under Pius IX and Leo XIII was not the ultimate criterion, the *quod semper, quod ubique, quod ab omnibus*. He was the prisoner in the Vatican library, for whom the papacy was the one unchanging fact: "the most conservative power in the world", the standard by which everyone was judged.[6]

This humourless, unimaginative and superficial history of the popes was a direct reflection of his convictions. Everything in his life centred on Rome, and he did not fear to write: *Romanus sum, Romani nihil a me alienum puto*. To yield its maximum, the *History* needs to be read in the light of his voluminous *Diaries*, where the servility of his attitude to authority is naïvely set down. He feels to order. "Today", he writes to his mother, after seeing Pius IX for the first time,

[6] The prejudice in favour of the papacy through which Pastor viewed the past is amply illustrated in his treatment of Diether von Isenburg; his shortcomings have been exposed in an article under that title by Cormac Rigby in *The Downside Review*, April 1963, pp. 125–141.

"Today is the happiest day I have known since my first communion." The violent emotion caused by the sight of the "eighty-four years old martryr-pope" is expressed in the most threadbare and conventional of pious phrases, the mediocrity of the man is disguised as the "sincerity" of the Catholic. The *Diaries* reveal an absence of spontaneity, freshness and humour which is that of a man whose emotional development has been arrested. Where facts were concerned he was usually honest, but the framework in which they were presented was never in question: the question of intellectual honesty does not arise. Emotionally, he was too underdeveloped; and his one form of indulgence was to assist at papal ceremonies: the baroque accoutrements of Vatican ceremonial impressed him as they did a peasant woman from the Abruzzi. He never reached the age of introspection, and the completeness of his reliance on authority placed him beyond criticism. Nothing which Kraus, von Hertling, Schell or the social Christians could say impressed him as other than insubordination, and he used the whole of his very considerable influence to silence them.

This singularly charmless example of the sacristy Catholic was much given to intrigue; and during the pontificate of Pius X he used his position to lay information and arouse suspicion against his adversaries. He did not scruple to get Duchesne excluded from the Pontifical Society for the Advancement of Learning. His method was that of the servant implanting suspicions in the mind of his master, without too direct an accusation, so that if necessary he could withdraw. With his close knowledge of the German Catholic world, his hyper-orthodoxy, his influential friends among the episcopate and aristocracy, he became a valuable go-between. Kraus intrigued to forward his own ideas; the notorious Mgr Benigni was a professional spy in the service of Merry del Val; von Pastor was a freelance informer who used his position and the honours which were showered upon him to oppose in private the ideas which in public he was careful to dissociate himself from, but which he never openly attacked. He exemplifies the difficulties which the reformers in Germany met with in arousing any sense of the urgency of the position. The Pastor *Diaries* are the key to strength of the ghetto, an invaluable memento of an atmosphere which few would defend.

Six months before von Hertling's speech Pastor had detected signs of "liberalism" as he passed through Munich, and noted in his *Diaries* that "we shall not be spared a struggle", though for him it would not be above board. When, six months later, he bought and read Hermann Schell's pamphlet *Catholicism the principle of progress*, he saw at once that his original fears had not been unfounded, and indeed that Schell's booklet was something new. Schell, he noted, is a far more dangerous phenomenon than "Spectator" (Kraus), for while Spectator writes on political matters, Schell deals with the religious sphere. Schell had gone to the heart of the matter, and though the professor of theology at Wurzburg had not the literary skill of Kraus, his aim was true and his frankness something approaching the brutal. His attack on "Romanism" and on servility towards authority might have been addressed to Ludwig von Pastor.

The pamphlet opens with an enumeration of the facts referred to by von Hertling, and gives the statistics showing the fall in the level of Catholic education. But these phenomena, he goes on to say, are merely the symptoms of the disease. The root of the evil is the "inferiority (of Catholics) in the independent use of their reason" and the want of independence which produces nothing but "spiritual eunuchs". This is directly attributable to the *romanische Geist*, to the Latin spirit, or as Kraus would have said, to the Guelfs who had imposed their system on Germany. "The Catholic spirit does not require that everything in religion should be Latin or medieval, but that a nation should be Christian." The authoritarian régime of Rome had kept Catholics minors;[7] they no longer dared to use their judgement, but referred in all matters to authority. This was no less fatal to the individual than to the authorities themselves, whose leadership was in fact a counterpart to the servility they exacted: they too had lost the power to judge, to trust their own instincts and consciences, and relied on external, extrinsic proofs: witness the case of Leo Taxil. A large part of Schell's pamphlet is taken up giving the facts of this, the most notorious hoax of the century, in which the Roman authorities, the official organ of the Jesuits, the *Civiltà cattolica* and a large number of the clergy in France and in Germany had been made to believe in the "revelations" of "Diana Vaughan", purporting to give detailed and horrific accounts of the Satanism practised in the Masonic Lodges.

The rest of his pamphlet, and of his reply to his opponents (*Der alte und der neue Glaube*) was concerned with the question of the education of the clergy, where he made good use of Manning's notes "Hindrances to the spread of Catholicism", and of the example of the Church in America. The views put forward are innocuous enough by present standards, and as regards the education of the clergy no less relevant; but the criticism of Rome could not be allowed to pass. Two years later, in 1898, Schell's books were put on the Index. He submitted at once, and died in 1906. His death was a blow to the reformers. It is true that the work he had begun was continued by other hands, but *Reformkatholizismus* never rose above the pamphlet, or the sectarian review (*Das neue Jahrhundert*, edited by Philipp Funk): it was a courageous protest against abuses, but it lacked the weight and the following to produce results. Ludwig Pastor remained the model of what he himself called "the strict Catholic", and as the Modernist Controversy developed in France any form of opposition to Rome was stamped "modernist" and killed.

[7] Cf. Blondel's reference to "perpetual minors", *op. cit.*, p. 106.

The unrest which Kraus, Hertling and Schell had shown to exist was not confined to the intellectual sphere, and the same stress and strain developed within the Centre party itself. During the ten years preceding the war of 1914, the Centre was divided into two groups: those who followed the progressive social views of München-Gladbach, supported by Julius Bachem and the *Kölnische Volkszeitung*; and the conservative wing based on the *Bauernverein* of the Rhineland. The former, returning to the original intentions of the founders of the Centre party, wished to collaborate with the Christian democratic parties, and to this end argued in favour of Christian as opposed to Catholic Trade Unions. The latter clung to the patriarchal conceptions of the past, and feared "interconfessionalism" no less than the industrialized society of the modern world. Each group sought and obtained the backing of Rome, which hesitated to pronounce on matters of which it was wholly ignorant, but feared still more to delegate its authority. The quarrels divided the Centre, and the reiterated appeals to Rome, publicized its dependence on the Vatican. The elections of 1912 revealed the unfavourable effects of the controversy. One of the leading members of the Centre, a priest from Baden, spoke out strongly, refuting the imputations of clericalism; but when his speech was printed it was condemned in Rome. Defeat at the polls demonstrated the weakness of the ghetto more effectively than any argument; but the problem was solved by very different means: the *Kulturkampf* mentality and the ghetto were engulfed by the chauvinism of the war period and finally swept away by the revolution which followed.

But in fact the liberation of Catholicism in Germany was to come, as it came in France, through men of letters and philosophers, and if any one man deserves to be named as the first in time it is Carl Muth, the founder of *Hochland*. When *Hochland*, "A periodical for all the fields of knowledge, literature and art" first appeared in 1902 it was a venture in unknown territory, into the free world of art, literature and criticism, which had been progressively abandoned since the decline of the romantic movement. Muth had the courage, the authority and flair that makes an editor, which enabled him to weld the contributors into a whole without sacrificing their individuality, and to pick out and foster an undeveloped talent. He made *Hochland* into a platform which was never allowed to fall into the hands of the partisan or the specialist, and his eclectic taste was a powerful civilizing and humanizing agent during the next decade, and served to prepare the ground for the future. From the first Muth's undertaking was frowned upon and there is an entry in Pastor's diary which expresses the ghetto view in a few words:

> The quarrel between Kralik and Muth turns on the same point, at bottom, as the quarrel between the supporters of the *Kölnische Volkszeitung* and its adversaries. The ones, and to these I belong, look for salvation in a courageous and frank confession of the Catholic point of view; the others, to which Muth belongs, believe in accommodating themselves to their opponents, and in extreme concessions. Between the two there can be no compromise.

The point which Pastor makes against Muth is exactly the same as his point against Schell: "The spiritual inferiority Schell talks about only occurs among us when we descend to the level of our opponents." "The Catholic point of view" to Pastor and his likes was a completed and closed system neither requiring nor tolerating any communication with the outside world. It was because Muth rejected this ghetto view of Catholicism that he was pursued by its defenders—among others by Mgr Benigni, Merry del Val's creature. But where it was easy to silence the theologian, and relatively easy to exert pressure on the politician, it was more difficult to control a literary journal. The attempt was, however, made, and failed when Muth refused to accept a censor appointed by Rome on grounds, which were readily understood, that he could not afford one.

When Muth was honoured, in 1927, with a *Festschrift*, both title and contents illustrate his achievement: *Widerbegegnung von Kirche und Kultur* would, in tone, content and level have been unthinkable twenty-five years earlier: Muth and *Hochland* had brought the Church and culture together again, or more accurately, he had made communication possible both by accustoming Catholics to open-minded discussion, and by gradually reducing their fear of using their reason responsibly. Muth, too, might have taken *Sapere aude* as his motto. He had seen, in his own way, that the alternative to political Catholicism was "religious Catholicism", which since it could not exist in vacuo, in a ghetto, must venture into the world through "all the fields of knowledge, literature and art". He did not want an aesthete's religion, but a religion which instead of being condemned to reaction could act and create. He had seen what Claudel had seen, that the crisis was the result of a starved imagination, which like vitamins cannot be weighed or measured, but is no less necessary.

But whereas the revival in France was a spontaneous return to the philosophy and ideas of the romantic movement (in Blondel, Bremond, Claudel and Péguy), the revival in Germany lacked the vitality either to rediscover them spontaneously or perceive its affinities with its older tradition. It was only very gradually that the importance and relevance of the Catholic romantics dawned on their heirs, partly because the romantic thinkers had gone out of fashion, partly because so recent a past is always difficult to see as a whole and in relation to the present; so that it was really only after the 1914 war that the Catholic revival in Germany became conscious of its historical position and its heritage.

The task before us [Philipp Funk wrote in *Hochland* in 1928] is to continue what was then begun, to take up anew what escaped them, to develop and work out the problems they left behind them. For if the present or the immediate past (i.e. the pre-war decade) can be reckoned a turning point, that is only so in so far as it is a wave of the turning point which occurred a hundred or a hundred and twenty years ago, breaking on our shores. However new the problems appear, however newly dressed up they may be, all of them need to be brought back to the basic problems engaging the men of those times, re-examined and simplified in that light.

Philipp Funk, who had sown his intellectual wild oats as editor of *Das neue Jahrhundert*, and who called himself the disciple of F. X. Kraus, was, I believe, one of the first to realize to the full the importance of the age of Sailer and the work of Möhler, of the Catholic renaissance described in the early sections of this essay. Since his time, as has been said, writers like Geiselmann and Dempf have shown the essential accuracy of his interpretations. What appeared in 1890 as movement of reform, ended as the rediscovery of tradition—not in the static form of the ultramontanes and Pastor—but as dynamically conceived by the romantics and by contemporary writers like Blondel in *Histoire et Dogme*. But, before this affinity could be perceived, it was necessary that the romantic renaissance itself should be brought to light and understood, and this was in the main the work of writers and critics outside the Catholic tradition.

The labour of excavation, of editing and re-editing the works of the romantics was begun by Dilthey, in his study of Schleiermacher and Schlegel. But it was the literary talent of Ricarda Huch, and her two volumes of studies on the romantics, which started, or at least determined, the swing of fashion. A real gift for *haute vulgarisation* revived interest in the lives and ideas of men whose way of thought came as a pre-echo of the vitalistic and evolutionary philosophies of Bergson and Simmel. In literature, the reaction against naturalism—the poetry of Maeterlink, of George and Rilke and the symbolists

—opened the way to mysticism; and largely through the perseverance of a bold publisher, Eugen Diederichs, the works of Eckhardt, Tauler, Suso, and Angelus Silesius were once again put before the reading public as in the days of Sailer. Among Catholics, the name of Joseph Bernhardt should be mentioned for his work in this connection—though as he himself says in his Memoirs, the men chiefly responsible were free-thinkers.

Until the war the revival of interest in the romantics and the mystics was literary and often superficial, but although the atmosphere was changing, the Catholic world was still immobilized in mediocrity. In 1911, however, Eugen Diederichs embarked on a project which, when the old world fell to pieces, was to magnetize the whole field, organize and orientate what had already been achieved, and provide a wholly new perspective. During the next six or seven years Diederichs published the complete works of an unknown Danish writer, and revealed the flashing genius of Sören Kierkegaard. The translation was indifferent, the editing tendentious, but the impression was indelible. No Christian writer since Pascal had written with the same burning passion, the same crystal integrity, fusing imagination and reflection, feeling and dialectics. Kierkegaard's work, and this was the most immediate cause of its influence, was written for a world in which—to quote the stereotyped phrase which he uses— "Christendom no longer exists"; and because that truth was ignored or denied for political reasons his last pamphlets were entitled "Attack on Christendom".

In Kierkegaard the spirit of Hamann, with whom the romantic philosophy in Germany begins, lived again, and this time supremely articulate. His double-barrelled polemic, against Christendom on the one hand and against the rationalized religion of Hegel on the other, placed him at the centre of the debates of the day. His existential thought shattered conventional apologetics as finally as Kant had shattered the rationalistic apologetics of Wolff—and his work did for

Catholicism in Germany something of the same order as that of Bergson and Blondel in France. He spoke for the whole man, and in defence of *le tout de l'homme*. Theodor Haecker, who translated his *Journals*, and made him known among a wider Catholic audience, owed his conversion to Kierkegaard.

Kierkegaard's work dropped like a *deus ex machina*, to provide the *dénouement* to a situation which had lacked the men of spirit and the circumstances to reach the penultimate state of crisis. But his advent was prepared by the meteoric career of Max Scheler as he passed through the Church. Scheler's conversion, while it lasted, conferred an inestimable benefit upon the Church in Germany which more than anything lacked a man of calibre, something other than a good academic mind. Scheler was a genuine thinker, capable of dominating the contemporary culture he had assimilated. His range was very considerable, his aim accurate. And as a Catholic he communicated—often through the pages of *Hochland*—his sense of the length, breadth and depth of the Catholic heritage to the rising generation, and a sense of independence and responsibility proper to mature men who had finished their education in the trenches. He had, moreover, the capacity as well as the standing to make himself heard outside the Church, and many of those who read him learnt for the first time that the Church was not an organization run from Rome, but the mystical body of Christ.

The nineteenth century ended (in the war of 1914) for Catholicism in Germany as it had begun, with a return to the ideals and ideas of Sailer, Schlegel and Möhler whose works, in return, became a source of rejuvenation. But whereas on the first occasion the romantic movement had outgrown its philosophical and theological roots, and had fallen a victim to the Roman policy of conducting the life of the Church as though Christendom were still a reality, on the second occasion the literary and aesthetic movement with which it began was pruned back by the harsh realities of the times, and the sap forced back into the roots. There was nothing spectacular in the post-war period, no poet to compare with Claudel, no writer to approach Péguy, no philosopher of the originality of Blondel. But if instead of the search for the signs and wonders of a renaissance one attends to the change in the ethos of Catholicism, the transformation was no less than in France, and the Church of Germany returned to its own traditions, and in so doing was re-integrated in the growing unity of the Church as a whole.

SELECT BIBLIOGRAPHY

THE only works in English on the Church in Germany are the essays of Lord Acton, in particular those contained in *Essays in Church and State* (London, Hollis and Carter, and New York, Viking Press, 1953); see also the essays on Döllinger in Acton's *History of Freedom* (1907) and the early pages of "German Schools in History" in *Historical Essays and Studies*, both published by Macmillan & Co.

French

GOYAU, Georges: *L'Allemagne religieuse*, Paris, Perrin, 1905; *Jean Adam Möhler*, Paris, 1906; *Bismarck et l'Église, le Kulturkampf*, two volumes, Paris, Perrin, 1911.

VERMEIL, Edmond: *J. A. Möhler et l'école de Tubingue*, Paris, Armand Collin, 1913.

German

BUCHHEIM, Karl: *Geschichte der Christlichen Parteien in Deutschland*, Kosel, 1953.

ESCHWEILER, K.: *J. A. Möhler's Kirchenbegriff*, Bramsberg, 1930; *Die Zwei Wege der Neueren Theologie*, Augsburg, 1926. Festschrift für Karl Müth: *Wiederbegegnung von Kirche und Kultur*, Kösel and Pustet, 1927.

FUNK, P.: *Von der Aufklärung zur Romantik*, Kösel and Pustet, 1925.

GEISELMANN, R.: *Von lebendiger Religiosität zum Leben der Kirche*, Stuttgart, 1952.

GROSCHE, Robert, and others: *Der Weg aus dem Ghetto*, Cologne, Verlag J. P. Bachem, 1956.

SCHNABEL, Franz: *Deutsche Geschichte im XIX Jahrhundert*, Volume III, part II, and Volume IV, Vienna, Herder, 1929.

One of the best books on German romanticism in any language is Albert Béguin's *Le Romantisme et le rêve*. On the central question touched on in Chapter IX and the problems facing the Church in the present age, Maurice Blondel's *La Semaine sociale de Bordeaux* (published under the pseudonym *Testis*) is the only thoroughgoing criticism of the philosophy behind the "thesis", and contains a brief statement of his own point of view.

.

The Twentieth Century Encyclopedia of Catholicism

The number of each volume indicates its place in the over-all series and not the order of publication.

All titles are subject to change.